M000042025

Physical Asset Management for the Executive

Copyright ©2008 Howard W Penrose, Ph.D.

All Rights Reserved. No part of this book may be reproduced in any form or by any electronic or mechanical means including information storage and retrieval systems—except in the case of brief quotations embodied in critical articles or reviews—without permission in writing from its publisher, SUCCESS by DESIGN Publishing.

Published By: SUCCESS by DESIGN Publishing
5 Dogwood Ln, Old Saybrook, CT 06475
Email: howard@motordoc.net

This publication is designed to provide accurate and authoritative information in regard to the subject matter covered. It is sold with the understanding that the use of the information contained within this book does not imply or infer warranty or guaranties in any form.

10-digit ISBN: 0-9712450-6-1
13-digit ISBN: 978-0-9712450-6-8

For Nick and Matt

This is for your future.

Table of Contents

Introduction

There are very few books written to discuss an important topic related to the success of our corporations, careers, and profitability for our business management and business schools–Physical Asset Maintenance and Management. Through a review of materials, coursework and textbooks, very little time or energy is spent in the identification and benefits of one of the single largest potential cost improvements for our organizations.

Based upon US Census Bureau statistics and a 1979 maintenance study performed by MIT, it was projected that the size of the reliability and maintenance industry in the USA was $1.2 Trillion in 2005 in which between $500 to $750 Billion was the direct cost of poor physical asset maintenance and management. Of the $12.5 Trillion Gross Domestic Product for the USA, at the time, an additional 20% was lost due to poor or improper physical asset maintenance and management while over 60% of businesses rely upon maintaining equipment reactively (repair when fail). In effect, up to $0.75 Trillion direct costs and $2.5 Trillion potential was lost in 2005.

This means that the combined direct and indirect potential for the USA, alone, ranked somewhere between the second and third largest economies of the world and more than twice the economy of Canada!

If we want to put this further into perspective, an area that has been focused on from the early 1980's through the present has been logistics, or the movement of materials. In 1985, the costs

Table 1: 2005 Top Ten Global GDP

Ranking	Country	2005 GDP in $Trillions
1	United States of America	$12.5
2	Japan	$4.5
3	Germany	$2.8
4	China	$2.2
5	United Kingdom	$2.2
6	France	$2.1
7	Italy	$1.7
8	Spain	$1.1
9	Canada	$1.1
10	Brazil	$0.8

associated with logistics were 16% of the GDP and by 2005 it was decreased by 5% to 11% of the USA GDP.

In the 1980's, the general business improvement opportunities were significant. The rise of the MBA had reached its peak and our business was focused more on the finance of business with the stock market driving more and more of our significant business decisions. This was the era of Jack Welch at GE, Eliyahu Goldratt's Theory of Constraints, and Hammer and Champy's concepts of Lean and Business Reengineering and other financial and business giants and concepts. We have applied these concepts and practices to our businesses for over 20 years and, after reaping the benefits of the initial improvements, continue to expend vast amounts of energy and resources in obtaining smaller and smaller improvements.

In our present climate, only minor adjustments and improvements have been made in facilities to make improvements to energy efficiency, as well. What is particularly interesting is that a combination of properly applied energy, reliability and maintenance improvements, even minor, will have a significant impact on the bottom line. The impact of just the 'low hanging fruit' will be significant in virtually every company globally at the time of the writing of this book.

As a Reliability and Maintenance (R&M) consultant, I have had the advantage of being able to enter any facility environment and identify low cost, high impact R&M improvements with the only concern being that I under-estimate the impact of the effect of the application of the recommendation. In every single case, the result of a recommendation, when implemented, has had paybacks measured in months, weeks, days, hours, minutes and even seconds after implementation. The question this has raised for me is: why do managers not realize the potential benefits of proper R&M programs?

The answers are simple, with two primary responses: R&M and management speak different languages; and, our education and experience within the organization does not help us identify the opportunities.

Where are we in our industry at this time? Let us consider the purchase of a new vehicle. You have, personally, made a significant investment in transportation and/or entertainment. There are things that you perform to keep the vehicle in a condition to reliably get you to and from your destination. One of those is a standard oil change every 3,000 miles, or so, with an oil filter change, lubrication, check the belts, and other inspections performed on the car. When the tires eventually begin to wear significantly, we may change them immediately, or keep a close eye on them to replace them so that we get maximum life out of them while planning time off or a weekend for the work. Brakes are checked on occasion to ensure that we are able to safely stop.

Now, if we consider how we run our facility and production assets, the scenario is quite different. We operate the plants trying to figure out how to not lubricate equipment. Perhaps we buy into automatic lubricators, which would be like using those synthetic oils they show on commercials where the car is drained and allowed to run until the engine burns up. Would it last as long as if it actually had the lubrication taken care of properly? We run production equipment full out, or to meet demand levels, even though signs of wear identify an eventual blowout, much like running on bald tires. When the tire(s) go, it is rarely at a convenient time. Or we wait until the brakes come apart and we cannot stop the vehicle. Yet, that is the way we are maintaining our equipment. Failing the engines and functions of our businesses because we perceive that it is cheaper than properly maintaining our equipment to reliably perform our business.

Would you want the maintenance department of the building you work in to not properly maintain the elevators that you take to your office? What happens if they maintain them the same way as your production equipment? If the motor fails, or the cable snaps, can you trust the brakes? How about aircraft? Aren't we starting to see an increase in maintenance related delays and news related to landing gear problems and other issues? The R&M industry impacts a great many parts of our lives. The next time we get on that elevator or get on that airplane, what if they are maintaining it the same way you maintain your facilities and production equipment? Would you want to ride?

The next greatest evolution of business improvement is the proper maintenance and management of the company's physical assets. The maintenance industry, as a whole, has been watching and trying to figure out how to communicate to management the importance of R&M on the bottom line. Unfortunately, due to the language barriers between maintenance and management, they need your help.

In this book, we are going to discuss means, methods and communications related to the R&M industry and how improvements can be made. These concepts are tried and true and applicable to companies from the very small to the very large. I have implemented these, or hybrids, of these concepts within a number of Fortune 100 companies with tremendous success. We are also going to spend time bridging the language gap, something our training and experience has not provided for us, by looking at cause-effect of our decisions related to R&M.

Chapter 1

The Culture and Impact of Maintenance

The common practice for R&M budget management is to continue to address the issue by reducing the budget each year. By the end of the year, the budget has been exceeded significantly and the maintenance manager is brought on the carpet.

At first I tried to understand why we in the R&M industry were so masochistic. The maintenance staff works hard, usually end up putting in overtime on weekends, holidays and have vacations cut short or cancelled. When I left the 'floor' and started into R&M (including energy) research I began to see the reason. Working in the boardroom, conference room, teaching and training have been exciting, but there is no greater 'rush' than solving a machine problem and getting production equipment back up and running. You see immediate results from your work and the satisfaction is addictive. Moreover, when equipment goes down and production is at a standstill, you get attention and may even be rewarded for how quickly you get the equipment back up and operating.

The effect has been referred to as 'Hero Maintenance.' It is often described as people not seeing the maintenance staff until something fails. Then all of a sudden these people come out of the woodwork with magic tools and the equipment starts, everything goes back to normal with the only comment being, 'who were those masked men?'

The challenge is that when R&M works properly, this type of situation should very rarely occur. In fact, improper maintenance is one of the issues that has brought us to these crossroads to begin with. When equipment was built like tanks, was very reliable and our workforce extremely confident, equipment failures did occur, but rarely. We maintained everything, whether the machines or structures were critical or not, because it made sense and cost was a minor issue. Everything else we just lived with.

In the 1980's, the primary focus within business became ways and means to reduce the cost of business, throughput and breaking production bottlenecks. The concept was to trim the fat of these companies by trying to eliminate unnecessary tasks and the reduction of personnel. However, a lack of training by those making the trimming decisions, and reengineering programs, caused the reduction of maintenance personnel. Part of the issue related to the reduction of personnel and maintenance programs is a simple rule of thumb: the full impact of a program is not felt for twelve to twenty-four months. This rule is known and holds true in business as well as within the maintenance organization.

Figure 1: Cost of Maintenance Strategies

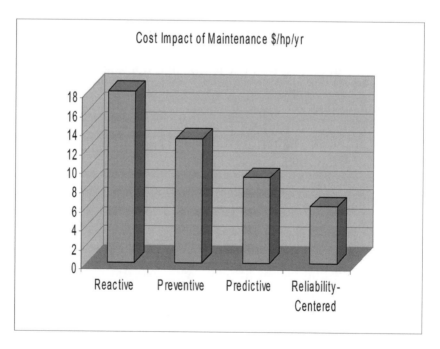

At the end of the 1980's and into the 1990's, senior management began to demand the same requirements for corporate projects of the R&M organization even while technology was finally at a point to improve the ability to 'predict' or estimate times to failure for machinery. The result was that maintenance personnel had to present business cases and justify work without the training to do so. The tools provided were 'cost avoidance' and 'simple payback.'

In the 1960's, the FAA worked with air carriers and manufacturers to develop the minimum maintenance requirements for aircraft. In the early 1970's the US Military contracted two reliability managers from United Airlines, Nowlan and Heap, to develop Reliability-Centered Maintenance (RCM) for weapons and aircraft. The document, published in 1976 as 'Reliability-Centered Maintenance,' was a public document that drove future maintenance program development within all branches of the military, in particular the 3-M (Materials Maintenance and Management) for the US Navy. Developing and implementing maintenance for military and US Coast Guard equipment requires training in RCM and a continuous improvement program referred to as the Maintenance Effectiveness Review, or similar names. Military personnel are trained to generate and follow specific planning and scheduling as well as detailed step-by-step maintenance processes. Most industrial maintenance programs have at least one military experienced personnel.

In the mid to late 1970's, newer testing technologies such as vibration analysis, hand-held electrical test equipment, ultrasonic equipment and more, began to enter the industry as non-destructive equipment. The use of the technologies accelerated towards the end of the 1980's and began to become more common in the 1990's. The benefit of such technologies has been the ability to detect different equipment defects without disassembly or interruption of production. However, these technologies require a great deal of training and experience for data interpretation. Additionally, the length of time between fault detection and equipment failure is generally difficult to predict by these personnel unless equipment failure history is readily available.

Maintenance knowledge tends to be handed down by word of mouth from an experienced technician to an 'apprentice,' or through trade or technical classes. Small changes to how maintenance is performed began to evolve over time such that inefficiencies and small changes developed based upon short cuts and work-arounds. For instance, proper lubrication of electric motor bearings has always required de-energizing the motor prior to adding a small amount of grease. With equipment not being shut down due to production requirements and a push to reduce overtime, bearings would be greased while the motors were running. Additionally, the position of 'oiler' or lubrication technician was replaced over time as it was assumed that lubrication did not require any significant skill. At some point in time, events occurred that propagated the change and added the concept of 'flushing' the bearings, or pumping grease until all of the old grease comes out of the bearing housing.

An example of how these changes occur happened in the 1990s in the Chicago area. In 1993 and 1994, a rash of bearing failures in belted applications occurred. We noticed this in the motor repair industry as the rate of failure was unusually high and tended to occur in commercial buildings. Finally, our team was brought in to review a catastrophic failure of a 75 horsepower motor in a commercial building. When we arrived, the wrench and six foot pipe used to tighten the adjustable base was still there and the belts had been tightened to the point where the shaft encroached into the bearing housing of the motor. When we traced it back further, it was discovered that a trainer teaching a class at a local High Voltage Air Conditioning (HVAC) school was teaching technicians to tighten belts by amp draw. The technicians were told to tighten the belts until the motor current met the nameplate value. To put this into perspective, most belted applications in commercial buildings are sized to about 50% of full load.

R&M professionals, be they maintenance technicians or reliability engineers, by and large have the goal of the company in mind: Keeping the assets up and running such that the company can produce product. They also must meet goals that are set for them, such as maintenance task completion and other R&M-related Key Performance Indicators (KPI). In many cases, in order to meet their goals as set forth with either paper or Computerized Maintenance and

Management Systems (CMMS), the maintenance staff must take over production equipment. Predictive and Condition-Based Maintenance recommendations are submitted with recommendations based upon the tools that management has given them—cost avoidance numbers—and the results, recommendations or generic findings are ignored. The result is a level of frustration only countered by the increasing number of catastrophic unplanned failures that provide the rush that we discussed earlier.

Chapter 2

Maintenance and Management

"Ninety-nine percent of all problems in communications start with misunderstandings which develop as a result of differing viewpoints and conditioning."

—Anonymous

The present issues associated with communication between maintenance and management are historical and not something that has just started, and can be seen in terms of centuries versus decades. The opinions and history of how things have developed differ based upon the point of view of the authors and intended audience. For instance, management books written by managers/ academics and associated with MBA training tend to have very little information related to physical asset maintenance, while maintenance books tend to have very little information on executive management. In fact, in reviews of MBA textbooks, only a few discuss maintenance at all, and those tend to be limited to a few paragraphs. Several others ignored the function of skilled trades and labor and, instead, focus on how to hold a hard position with unions for negotiations. Most R&M training and books focus on how to present dollar savings and 'value added' information as the method of communicating with management.

In effect, both the R&M professionals and business professionals are being trained and educated into a communication gap problem! This shows, quite often, in the frustration levels of both maintenance and management concerning each other.

2.1 Guilds and Unions

The organization of labor practice is credited to Numa Pompilius, King of the Romans, who united musicians, carpenters and other artisans in 714-652 BC for the benefit of the community. This involved a trust that the people who requested work or services of the artisans would be guaranteed that they had the appropriate credentials.

For millennia prior to the industrial revolution, most people worked for themselves. As a result, they fashioned their own communities, which were later referred to as guilds in Europe, but had variations within all major countries from early times. Up through the middle ages, the guild increased in power, politically and economically, and provided insurance of quality and workmanship. With the expansion of the guild came the introduction of the middle class and the feudal system of Europe.

The guild structure ensured that craftsmen were selected and trained by a master craftsman over a long length of time. The guilds protected their crafts by being allowed to hold their own courts and punishment of their own membership while also providing shelter and a means of finding new work within the guildhalls. The guilds also provided a set of rules and requirements that protected quality, workmanship and the individual craftsmen, for instance artists were only allowed to paint during daylight hours and only in areas that were well lit. In these times, the master craftsmen and journeymen were the business owners contracted through the guildhalls to perform projects.

With the beginning of the First Industrial Revolution, the security of the worker, or craftsman, began to shift from individuals banding together to groups of workers working for a single company. This evolution occurred gradually, but significantly enough to change traditions that dated back millennia.

The First Industrial Revolution is estimated to have begun from 1750 to 1830 in Great Britain following rapid changes to the textile industry in 1740 relating to woolen garments. In 1793, the Industrial Revolution accelerated with the invention of the cotton gin by Eli Whitney in the USA.

The First Industrial Revolution blended in with the second revolution around 1850 when technology and economic progress gained momentum with the development of steam-powered ships and the railway. The improvement in transportation made mass production for a larger market a reality.

Thomas Savery constructed and patented the 'Miners Friend' steam powered low-lift water pump in 1698. This device utilized steam at 8 to 10 atmospheres producing about one horsepower of pumping power. It did not use pistons or cylinders and, therefore, was not considered a steam 'engine.' In 1712, Thomas Newcomen patented a piston and cylinder system that operated above atmospheric pressure and produced approximately five horsepower. This device was also used for pumping systems in mining applications.

James Watt patented the first real steam engine in 1776, which led to the development of the steam engine and steam ships. Steam power was also used as a method to produce local power and was instrumental in the development of more powerful machine tools such as the lathe, planning and shaping machines. This, again, allowed the building of bigger and more powerful engines impacting material transportation worldwide.

Later, towards the end of the nineteenth century, transportation and power improved even further with the development of the internal combustion engine and electrical power distribution. The DC, then later, AC electric motor, generator and distribution system accelerated production and manufacturing even more in the 20th Century.

Through all of these massive changes, labor and management had their struggles. In December of 1869, with changes to work and labor, an illegal, secret group started known as the Knights of Labor. This organized group worked towards the development of an eight-hour workday, the end of child labor and equal pay for equal work. The principles of the Knights were based upon Freemason concepts and rules. In 1886, the Knights of Labor lost their craft labor to the American Federation of Labor (AFL) and was non-existent by 1900.

The AFL was founded by Samuel Gompers in 1886 as a national federation of skilled workers' unions. The Committee for Industrial

Organizations (CIO) was created by John Lewis in 1933 and split for the AFL in 1938 to merge again in 1955 as the AFL-CIO. In the meantime, other unions, including the United Auto Workers (UAW), which was founded in 1935, mining unions, transportation unions and, later, company and government unions were developed.

The unions represented the same basic principles as the guilds of the past, including safety and power in numbers. The strength and power of these unions was tested, and established, with the 1936 UAW strikes in Flint, Michigan where workers locked themselves in while bargaining for a safer workplace, better wages, benefits and a slowdown of the push towards a much faster pace of assembly.

In general, since the 1800's, the strength and power of unions have increased and decreased based upon general social feelings towards unions and business and government intervention.

2.2 Business Management and Manufacturing

In 1824, John Hall, Chief Engineer of Harpers Ferry Armory, developed a method of manufacturing muskets with inter-changeable components. In 1828, large-scale manufacturing of muskets using specialized machine tools and, primarily, lesser skilled machinists was implemented at the armory. This marked a specific divergence of the requirement for skilled and unskilled labor, reducing costs for the development of weapons coupled with the ability to provide replacement parts. The workforce was then split between the unskilled workforce (direct workforce) that operated machines and a skilled workforce (indirect workforce) who maintained, repaired, setup and built the machines used by the laborers.

Over time, this progress was brought into industry even though the implementation of the processes and special-purpose machinery philosophy had significant impact on volume without a sacrifice of quality. Between 1860 and 1885, for instance, McCormick of Chicago increased production of agricultural equipment from roughly 4,000 machines per year to almost 50,000. Singer, from 1856 to 1885 increased its annual production of sewing machines from roughly 2,500 per year to over half a million. Most of the time taken to make changes to the production systems was overcoming the craft culture within each company.

In 1878, Frederick Taylor began his work in developing a process that he established and published in 1911: Scientific Management. The concept behind this new philosophy was to achieve machine-like standards of speed and reliability at all levels within the company. The task of the scientific manager was to study the workers, determine the simplest and fastest way for their work to be done and set a standard time for performance. The concept was that the processes within each organization would be completely automatic and so simple that training would be at a minimum and very little decision making would be required.

In the first decade of the 20th Century, over 20 percent of the labor force was comprised of children aged 10 through 15. At the time, the life expectancy of men was 46.3 years and 48.3 years for women. Additionally, with a large influx of immigrants, unemployment remained about 15%, leaving the power of employment with the employers. If working conditions were dirty, dangerous or otherwise unsatisfactory, the worker did not have a choice as others were always waiting for their position. During this decade, there was also a strong anti-union sentiment politically and socially.

By 1913, the Department of Labor was formed, split from the Department of Commerce, and the Federal Trade Commission was formed, which monitored companies in relation to the 1890 Sherman Antitrust Act. In 1911, Taylor published his work on Scientific Management, which was adopted by Henry Ford in his Highland Park plant in 1913. This application, using the manufacturing line and the time-based concept of 'speed up,' reduced the time to manufacture a vehicle from over 12.5 hours to just under 93 minutes. The government pushed harder on anti-trust work against such companies as Standard Oil and the American Tobacco Company.

From 1900 through 1920, the concept of the mega-business that could hire large numbers of unskilled labor and produce significant amounts of items cheaply was the goal of most business. Business had little to no focus on labor with comfort and safety concepts implemented incidentally to other business efforts. Through this period, it was generally felt that workers were motivated solely by economic incentives. Towards the end of this period, industry mobilized for war in 1916 and the USA entered World War I in 1917. Protectionist tariffs were implemented in 1913 in an effort to protect USA business followed by the first income taxes since the Civil War.

During the 'roaring 20s,' businessmen were viewed as 'superstars.' By 1923, General Motors implemented ideas on offering choices to consumers and, by 1926, took automotive leadership away from Ford, who stood behind the principle of customers having their choice of colors, 'as long as that choice was black.' Unemployment during this period dropped to 5.2 percent while immigration was restricted. The focus within business, at this time, was the customer and service.

From 1911 to the 1940s, the primary push was to develop tools and methods to reduce the time to manufacture products. The worker and craftsman lost his power to management, who assumed control over processes and quality. The loss of control began taking its toll on the concept of rewarding improvements and work volume that Taylor espoused, as his concepts of speed-up required a financial incentive.

From 1923 to 1933, a series of studies was commissioned by Western Electric out of Cicero, Illinois. The studies, known as the Hawthorne Studies, identified how work groups provide mutual support and resistance concerning management to unreasonably increased output. The research discovered that people had different needs than just money, they required acceptance by their co-workers.

The traditional assumptions, prior to the Hawthorne Studies, were:

- People try to satisfy one class of need at work: economic need;
- No conflict exists between individual and organizational objectives;
- People act rationally to maximize rewards; and,
- We act individually to satisfy individual needs.

The Human Relations Assumptions:

- Organizations are social systems, not just technical economic systems;

- We are motivated by many needs;
- We are not always logical;
- We are interdependent; our behavior is often shaped by the social context;
- Informal working group is a major factor in determining attitudes and performance of individual workers;
- Management is only one factor affecting behavior; the informal working group often has a stronger impact;
- Job roles are more complex than job descriptions would suggest; people act in many ways not covered by job descriptions;
- There is no automatic correlation between individual and organizational needs;
- Communication channels cover both logical/economic aspects of an organization and feelings of people;
- Teamwork is essential for cooperation and sound technical decisions;
- Leadership should be modified to include concepts of human relations;
- Job satisfaction will lead to higher job productivity; and,
- Management requires effective social skills, not just technical skills.

In the 1960s, business as a profession became accepted with the growing popularity of the MBA (Masters of Business Administration). By the 1970s, large business focus began to change from the consumer, by the boardroom, to investors and dividends. From the 1940s through to the 1980s, the mega-corporation (conglomerate), or corporations that buy out other companies whether they are part of the core business, or not, became the direction of business. During this time, it was expected that if you joined a company, you worked for them for life.

With the Theory of Constraints, job security became less sure around the 1980s, and dramatically less secure when General Electric started their turnaround in the 1990s. During this time period, from the mid-1980s, the generation of profit by divesting personnel and poorly operating divisions became the accepted norm.

The concepts of speed-up and lean manufacturing/lean office (re-engineering) continued to push the 'now' requirement into the

1990s and early 21st Century. Quarterly numbers, for large business, and short-term gains appear to hold sway over long-term plans and strategy. This issue is re-enforced as business schools are shortening the amount of time to complete an MBA as incentive to take their particular programs with a few advertising an MBA in as little as 12 months.

2.3 The Application of CMMS/EAM in R&M Communication

The introduction of Computerized Maintenance Management Systems (CMMS), in the 1980s, and Enterprise Asset Management (EAM) software at the end of the 1990s and into the 2000s, provided the concepts of Scientific Management to the Reliability and Maintenance (R&M) industry. The potential benefits to the application of CMMS/EAM are tremendous, when properly selected, applied, implemented and supported.

A properly applied CMMS system has the potential to provide information related to maintenance, parts, scheduling and other functions more effective while EAM systems have more potential to provide this functionality combined with communication with other systems, such as accounting. Additionally, a fully applied system can be used to provide the necessary information for Condition-Based Maintenance (CBM) processes such as Reliability-Centered Maintenance (RCM).

However, a majority of systems that have been implemented, worldwide, have not been effective. In effect, while the vendors state that there are tremendous savings to be realized, fewer than 8% of CMMS/EAM customers have realized those savings following millions of dollars and years to implement. In most of the applications that I have seen, whole new Information Technology (IT) departments are formed and consultants hired to maintain the CMMS/EAM programs. Is the balance of purchasing systems, the cost of skilled IT workers and consultants, as well as the other implementation costs, of value to the organization?

Most CMMS/EAM systems are Commercial-Off-The-Shelf (COTS) items. This basically means that one of the concepts that are hard to accept is that you must change how you do business in order to match what the vendor feels are 'best practices.' These best practices are usually formed around the financial portion of the business and tend to put CMMS/EAM floor-level practices as a last thought.

In effect, to be successful, the business and maintenance organization must change the way they do business. At this point more than half of businesses would have to perform major changes in how they do business in order to conform to the selected CMMS/EAM best practices. So far as the maintenance practice portion of the systems, most rely upon the user to develop the PM's (Preventive Maintenance) procedures. Therefore, if a company suffers from poor maintenance practices, the CMMS/EAM will simply automate the impending disaster.

Skilled trades and R&M professionals often view CMMS/EAM systems with suspicion. In the past, the skilled tradesman was a firefighter with a majority of their business being reactive repairs. The ego of the R&M professional was fulfilled with the victory of each 'save' of equipment and process. With a greater financial view of the company, upper level managers realized that an average of 40% of the cost of their business was related to the R&M effort. As a result, those corporate managers re-enforced decisions to implement CMMS/EAM strategies, but, as is often the case, leave the R&M departments with few resources, let alone input, into the selection and implementation of the systems.

With very little support and buy-in, many resist the application of the programs. In fact, many view the application with suspicion, concerned that 'big brother' is watching over their every action. In the meantime, maintenance management relies upon the accuracy of the CMMS/EAM system to provide accurate information to perform the tasks at hand. Executive management views the application of a software package to maintain and monitor the costs associated with maintenance. However, one of the most common issues with the application of the newer EAM systems, and in many cases, the CMMS systems, is the selection without regard to the actual application by maintenance.

The resistance is a double-edged sword for the maintenance organization. Management relies upon the CMMS/EAM system to provide information for allocating resources. In one of an increasing series of common occurrences, I was performing a site industrial survey. During the evaluation of the powerhouse of the site, I asked how they utilized the corporate CMMS system. The powerhouse maintenance supervisor, a skilled tradesman, proudly showed how effective his maintenance program was. However, he warned that the program was decaying because management was rapidly cutting the number of people. He had just dropped another five and did not know how he was going to meet his planned maintenance goals. I then inquired about how their times were reflected in the CMMS system. He stated, simply, that he felt that the use of the CMMS program was to force them to do things too fast and to monitor their work, so he did not use it and did not promote its use. They received their materials through common blanket purchase orders and only used the CMMS to process emergency work orders for repairs (i.e.: motor rewind and major pump repairs). When some of the repairs were not as critical, instead of sending them out, they would repair them in-house.

In this instance, management was unaware of the number of hours that were required to maintain the powerhouse and were reducing personnel via attrition, in such a way that met their union agreement requirements. The supervisor was unaware of the impact, had an ingrained paranoia about the use of the system and had not been trained in its use and benefits. I have seen enough of these to know that chances are good that the management attitude fed into the paranoia, which was re-enforced with the knowledge that the local manager-in-charge and the corporate managers-in-charge were unaware of this massive breakdown in the system.

In another survey, I sat in a maintenance meeting where a combined management and worker team discussed plant maintenance issues. I was impressed until the managers sent out the tradesmen and commenced to discuss the status of their facility in preparation for a report to corporate. Using red-yellow-green charts, they scored themselves 'green' on their CMMS implementation. During the survey, with a skilled trade acting as the guide, I noted that all of the CMMS terminals were locked, even though the philosophy was that anyone should be able to enter a work order. He laughed and explained that there had been no training, to date, and that most of the equipment was still not included in the system, even though the program had been in the plant for close to five years. The system was being used for planned maintenance and parts only. At the corporate location, I discovered that they were under the impression that the CMMS had been fully implemented.

As a third case, in an EAM application, during a site survey, the maintenance manager was proud of his percentage of completed PM's. During the walk-through I noticed a number of issues including: broken equipment that had not been entered into the EAM, and, the maintenance force concentrated on smaller non-critical PM's first, in order to keep the completion rate up. The company's reward system focused on completed PM's as recommended by their EAM implementation consultant.

During a site survey, performed prior to meeting with the plant supervisor as he was on vacation, I noted a high rate of leaking pump seals in process pumps (actually, it was a rate of 100% of all of the pumps). There were systems of water hoses pouring water over the pump shafts in order to keep the product from damaging the shafts or getting into the motor bearings (although the water was!). When brought to the maintenance manager's attention, he pulled up a work order screen on his CMMS system and announced that he only had a few pump seal work orders and that it couldn't be that bad. I walked through just one building and took pictures of over 65 pumps that were leaking product onto the floor and passageways. When presented, he was shocked that there were so many. It later turned out that the purchasing department, based upon the high rate of seal failures (average life of 18-24 months) decided to save money by changing from double to single seal cartridges. While reducing the cost by approximately half, they also reduced the seal life to about 4-6 weeks per seal. The maintenance staff, already burdened by a primarily reactive program, gave up entering work orders for the pumps.

In the development of motor system maintenance and management programs, one of the more important aspects required in order to effectively use the workforce is a good equipment history. In several ongoing corporate programs for Fortune 100 companies, in order to implement the programs parallel asset management software is usually required. These systems are used because almost all CMMS/EAM systems lack the details necessary for specific asset components, their repair histories, acceptance data, CBM findings and other details required for proper R&M practices that are related to root-cause-analysis, troubleshooting and other corrective and reactive maintenance practices. The unfortunate result, unless a modification allowing a link between systems is developed, is the requirement for parallel data entry.

One of the issues that will be discussed later in the book includes the inability for such systems to be flexible enough for CBM inspections and testing. A proper and effective CBM program requires flexibility in changing dates and details required for each inspection and/or test. For instance, the inspection of a filter may identify that while there is still useful filter life a closer inspection frequency may be required, briefly, until it is determined that the filter requires changing. With most CMMS/EAM systems wanting exact frequencies (i.e.: monthly, weekly, quarterly, etc.), this becomes very difficult. The result is that the filter is replaced too early or too late.

Finally, during a study on the impact of electrical motor diagnostics, we compared the detection of potential faults to the records of sixteen site locations. The very first thing that stood out from the evaluation of 8-10 months of records was that the information was extremely inaccurate. The extreme at one end was that virtually no work orders had been entered into the system by one site, where we were intimately aware of numerous issues, and the other extreme where every detail of daily maintenance was entered into the system. The good news, for us, was that the results were very conservative and that we knew our success numbers were very high. The bad news was that we were also involved in successful combined maintenance/management RCM and Maintenance Effectiveness Reviews (MER) that relied upon this data for success. We were now aware that the data that we needed to rely upon was completely unreliable and that our RCM and MER success rate could be much higher.

Chapter 3

Skilled Workforce
in the 21st Century

While demand for manufactured product has remained constant, or grown, as a share of the US economy, the actual production has lagged by a widening margin since 2000. This wedge means that actual demand has not translated to expanded employment output. Additionally, as the baby-boom generation grows older and leaves the workforce, there is a lag in replacement workers to cover the replacement demand and demand for new employment.

Figure 2: Manufacturing Labor in the USA (All Labor)

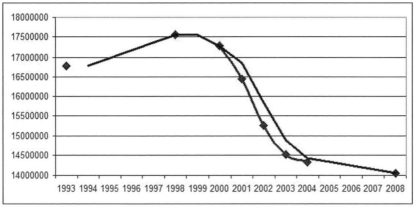

3.1 What Has Brought Us Here?

Baby boomers that were born from 1946 to 1964 will be between 50 and 68 years old in 2014. The annual growth rate of the 55 and older age group is projected to be 4.1%, four times the rate of growth of the overall labor force. The 25 to 54 age group will be around 0.3% and below 25 years will be essentially flat from 2004 through 2014. This means that our experienced and reliable workforce will be aging with a growing lag from a younger work force.

"Since the second decade of the 1900s, several population events have occurred in the United States with a long-lasting impact on future labor markets. The impact of these events appeared after a roughly 16 year lag, when the population cohorts involved entered the labor force."[1] The events in question are as follow:

1. 1920s and 1930s: A noticeable reduction in birthrates, a phenomenon referred to as the 'Birth Dearth.' This group presently makes up the 75-year and older generation, and is by and large, out of the workforce.
2. 1946 to 1964: The 'Baby-Boomer' era involved a significant increase in the US fertility rate and approximately 78 Million people were born. This segment was between the ages of 40 and 58 in 2004 and will be between the ages of 50 and 68 years in 2014.
3. 1965 to 1976: The 'Baby-Bust' era refers to the era where the number of births decreased once again. This segment of the population constitutes the prime-aged worker group aged 25 to 54 from 2004 through 2014. This group makes up a much smaller population and the difference in numbers will contribute to the decrease in the growth of the labor force through 2014.
4. 1976 to 2000: The 'Baby-Boom Echo' is comprised of the children of the baby-boomers after 1976. A part of this cohort en-

---

[1] Toosi, Mitra, "Labor Force Projections to 2014: Retiring Boomers," *Monthly labor Review*, US Census Bureau, November 2005.

tered the workforce in 2004 and will be in the prime-aged workforce by 2014.

As a result of this fluctuation in population, the baby-bust generation is entering the prime labor age. Because of the much smaller group, the numbers applied to replacing the aging workforce, as well as new job growth, will cause difficulty in the workforce by 2014.

The median age for the labor workforce peaked at 40.6 years in 1962. In 1982 this value was 35 years, 37.7 years in 1994, 40.3 in 2004 and is projected to be 41.6 in 2014. It is expected that labor growth will slow to 1% from 1.2% from 2004 to 2014. Additionally, the continued trend in 'early retirements' of the 55 and older workforce will signify additional challenges, especially as the early group of baby-boomers are already close to retiring in vast numbers.[2]

3.2 What is the Impact?

Defining the impact of this change is a challenge as it is meeting a range of responses from the Department of Labor Statistics, US Department of Defense, a variety of states' Departments of Commerce, and the National Association of Manufacturers, to name a few.

In a report presented by the US Department of Defense to Congress in February, 2005,[3] it was reported that there is no industrial crisis and that feelings of crisis are 'misplaced.' The report then goes on to justify why the US Department of Defense needs to obtain military materials overseas.

The US Bureau of Labor Statistics states, within its November 2005 report that while there is a change in the makeup of the workforce to an older workforce, that there is sufficient manpower to maintain USA competitiveness. However, all of the reports take into account number of people and not skill, experience or work ethic.

---

[2] Toosi, Mitra
[3] US Department of Defense, *Annual Industrial Capabilities Report to Congress*, February, 2005.

Figure 3: Change in Workforce (in 1,000's) by Age Group from 2004-2014

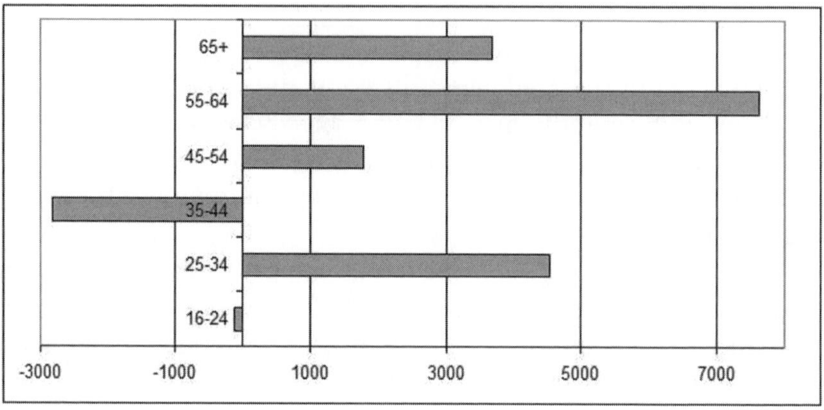

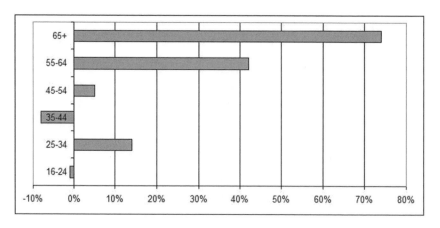

Figure 4: Percent Change in Workforce 2004-2014

The Wisconsin Manufacturing Study[4] identifies one of the key issues over the next decade will be the waning of a competent replacement workforce (Table 2).

---

[4] The MPI Group, *The Wisconsin Manufacturing Study: An Analysis of Manufacturing Statewide and in Wisconsin's Seven Economic Regions,* Wisconsin Manufacturing Extension Partnership, September 2005.

Table 2: Most Prominent Concerns 2005 to 2015

Concerns	Percent
Availability of skilled, qualified workers	61.6
Healthcare coverage and costs	19.2
Training	5.5
Compensation to workers and compensation levels	5.5
General benefits and insurances	2.7
All other	5.5

In the Spring of 2005, the National Association of Manufacturers contracted Deloitte to study the workforce.[5] "The details behind the talent shortage reveal a stark reality. More than 80 percent of respondents indicated that they are experiencing a shortage of qualified workers overall—with 13 percent reporting severe shortages and 68 percent indicating moderate shortages. Also worrisome is the finding that 90 percent of respondents indicated a moderate to severe shortage of qualified skilled production employees, including front-line workers, such as machinists, operators, craft workers, distributors, and technicians. As expected, the research showed that engineers and scientists are in short supply, with 65 percent of manufacturers reporting deficiencies—18 percent severe and 47 percent moderate."

What would cause this diverse view of the United States workforce over the next decade?

3.3 The Younger Generation

The four sets of information presented in this chapter are differentiated by their points of view. The US Bureau of Labor Statistics focus on the forecast of significant increase (about 60% of growth) in the professional and service industries, with the most significant being in the computer industry.

---

[5] Deloitte, *2005 Skills Gap Report—A Survey of the American Manufacturing Workforce*, NAM, Spring 2005.

"Advances in manufacturing technology, such as faster machines and more automated processes, and a shift of assembly and other production activities to countries with lower labor costs are expected to decrease employment for a number of production-related occupations."[6]

In particular, maintenance in the manufacturing industry is expected to decrease by 17,000 jobs with self-employment in this group increasing slightly. The total percentage of workforce in the maintenance and repair industry is expected to remain steady at 3.9%, although with a much-aged workforce. The US Bureau of Labor Statistics lists maintenance skilled workers as requiring moderate on-the-job-training (OJT) (e.g., farming and agriculture is long OJT and food service is short OJT).

In general, over the 2004 to 2014 period, 54.7 million job openings are expected in the economy, approximately three times as from general employment growth (18.9 million). The slower increase in population and available workforce is expected to fill in these jobs.

However, statistics do not account for the attitude of the 16 to 24 year old range, which is decreasing its presence in the workforce. "During the past several decades, the number of students enrolled in high school, college and summer school has increased, resulting in a decline in the overall labor force participation rate of youths, especially those 16 to 19 years. According to research by the Bureau of Labor Statistics, more of the workforce in the 16 to 24 year old age group reported going to school as one of the main reasons for their nonparticipation in the labor force in 2001 than their counterparts had reported a decade earlier."[7]

"The most disturbing barrier, manufacturers report, to securing needed workers is the broken image of manufacturing within the

---

[6] US Department of Labor Statistics, "Employment Outlook 2004–2014: Occupational Employment Projections to 2014," *Monthly Labor Review*, November, 2005.
[7] Toosi, Mitra

state. High school students disdain this future, avoid even discussing it with their colleagues, and accept manufacturing jobs apparently with reluctance."[8]

The incoming workforce, depended upon by the Bureau of Labor Statistics and US Department of Defense reporting of a lack of industrial crisis, is viewed differently by manufacturers. "There is an emerging two-tiered workforce in Wisconsin.[9] Older, reliable, hard-working employees are retiring soon. Their potential replacements may not be as dedicated to the work ethics of their forerunners and they are increasingly difficult to hire and retain."[10] The report continues to point out that although declining and replacement workers are not yet in high demand, the warning signs are there.

The issue in the USA is almost unique, as it relates to the 16 to 24 year generation. "The problem for US manufacturers is that the challenge is not universal. Countries with rich educational heritages, e.g., India, China and Russia, are graduating millions more students each year from college than the United States. With such international talent readily available and significant shortages existing at home, it is clear that the future of American manufacturing may now be at stake."[11]

Additionally, the quality of education and worker will be, and may presently be, degrading. "In addition to shortages of various types of employees, manufacturers surveyed reported that they are also dissatisfied with the skills of their current employees. Among respondents to this national survey, nearly half indicated their current employees have inadequate basic employability skills, such as attendance, timeliness and work ethic, while 46% reported inadequate problem-solving skills, and 36% indicated insufficient reading, writing and communication skills."[12]

---

[8] The MPI Group
[9] Note: Similar comments in studies within other USA State-funded research.
[10] The MPI Group
[11] Deloitte
[12] Deloitte

3.4 Connecting the Dots

The US Census Bureau, US Bureau of Labor Statistics and US Department of Defense each identify that the aging workforce is not an issue and no industrial crisis exists, even stating that such feelings of crisis are 'misplaced.' From a statistical point of view, this may appear realistic. However, the US Bureau of Labor Statistics did identify a dramatic change in the development of new jobs. Over 60% of new growth will be split between the higher income, higher education professional and management positions and the lower income, lower education servicing industry. Almost all other industries will be fairly stagnant.

Key industries, particularly in manufacturing, that make up the US middle class are moving, slowly, out of the USA. The US Department of Defense, which makes up less than 3.9% of the economy, is making purchasing decisions outside of the US manufacturing industry. Traditionally strong industries, such as automotive and steel, are quickly becoming commodities.

State Commerce departments and US manufacturers have identified a reluctance of the 16 to 24 year generation from entering industry, a reduced work ethic, challenges in retaining the younger workforce and difficulty obtaining skilled workers. "Clearly, this situation is untenable for America. Although our manufacturing sector has been able to remain vibrant and to compete successfully in a global economy, its ability to do so in the future is predicated on the availability of a highly skilled, innovative, 'high-performance workforce.' Without a sufficient supply of these types of employees, the manufacturing sector will suffer—which in turn will have a detrimental impact to the nation's overall economic health."[13]

3.5 Is There a Skilled Trades Crisis?

So far as maintaining the status quo, there is a skilled trades crisis, but not a lack of manpower, as supported by all of the studies and

---

[13] Deloitte

reports reviewed in this study. The present methods of doing business, including reliability and maintenance (R&M) tasks and procedures are similar to those concepts developed since 1824 at Harpers Ferry Armory and reinforced in 1911 by Frederick Taylor and his concepts of Scientific Management.

Since the development of the assembly line by Henry Ford in 1913, the effort has been to speed up production. Initially, the impact was the reduction of time in assembling a car from over 20 hours to less than 90 minutes. Through to the present day, time and motion studies, incentives, lean programs, reengineering, Theory of Constraints (TOC) and more, have been used to shave seconds off of manufacturing times.

Training, time limits, scheduling and technology have been applied to reduce R&M times. The attempted addition of Condition-Based Maintenance (CBM), EAM/CMMS software, budget cuts and more, have been used to reduce maintenance costs. However, studies have shown that over 90% of maintenance programs to not deliver as promised, over 57% of EAM/CMMS programs do not meet expectations and a European study reports that 92% of ERP systems do not meet expectations. A majority of maintenance programs return to chaotic reactive maintenance programs following attempts to apply planned maintenance and CBM programs.

In 1983, Eliyahu Goldratt introduced the Theory of Constraints. The purpose was to improve throughput and to reduce costs and inventories by reducing and removing constraints in the system. The concept of reduced costs being shown as reduced manpower was re-enforced. The application of Reengineering and Lean programs pushed this concept further, again. One of the key areas that management observed as a cost opportunity has been maintenance, which is an average of 40% of the operations budget of most facilities. In general, R&M was seen as an opportunity to reduce personnel that did not have immediate impacts.

With the entrance of the baby boom era into the workforce, there was an influx of readily available workers and an understanding that apprenticeships were required to bring R&M trades up to speed. This large number of readily available workers and trades, coupled with the application of automation and further reductions in time and motion, skilled wages increased slowly with management continuing to take further control of the workplace, a process initiated in 1824.

In the 1990s, some businesses, trade associations and professional societies begin to realize potential changes to the workforce as it becomes harder to find experienced workers in engineering and maintenance. Following 2000, the availability of an experienced and skilled workforce appears to have stagnated as the existing workforce advanced in age and the baby bust workforce just started into the workforce.

While it is also expected that there will be a slowdown in workforce growth, with the projected change to industry and manufacturing, it is expected that there will be enough replacement workers to manage existing and growth requirements. In fact, it is expected that through 2014, there will be a reduction for industrial and manufacturing skilled trades requirements by about 17,000.

The critical issue put forth by industry and manufacturing, per all of the studies, including the ReliabilityWeb.com survey, is the lack of a ready-to-work skilled workforce. The industrial and manufacturing studies primarily put the demand on academia and government to change training requirements to meet their needs. The lack of excitement, per many of the studies, by the 16-25 year-old generation, with the majority of new workers taking R&M positions as a last choice, is also an issue. Industry and manufacturing places the blame squarely on the younger generation, their parents, teachers and guidance counselors while not opening up the apprenticeships necessary to train the new workers. Finally, industry and manufacturers identify a lack of work ethic by younger workers and challenges hiring and retaining them.

3.6 What Can Be Done if the Present Direction is Maintained?

If we are to treat the change to the existing workforce as a crisis, the recommendations of many existing business studies can be considered good, with some compiling. These recommendations are as follow:

✔ Students, parents and teachers should be recommending skilled trades careers as a choice to students;

✔ Government should require traditional and trade schools to generate curriculum to meet local business requirements in skills, experience and work ethic;

✔ Government should support industry and manufacturing in the cost of apprenticeships; and,

✔ Workers should strive to multi-skill and identify their training needs to become more employable.

Additional requirements would include tort reform, additional protections for companies as incentives to generate apprenticeship positions, keep the economy strong and similar recommendations.

3.7 Who Is Responsible for Tackling the Skilled Workforce Issue?

The general trend of many of the business studies is for the responsibility to rest on government, academia and parents to promote and train the skilled workforce. This comes after decades of a lack of apprenticeships, R&M budget cuts, personnel cuts, long hours, lack of recognition and a lack of defined career paths by industry and manufacturing, in general.

Academia is also a business. In order to be successful, it must show a high job placement success rate upon graduation. If the jobs are not readily available, it is not in academia's interest to provide instruction that will not be attended or does not result in job placement.

Should government intervene and attempt to maintain the status quo? In the case of some industries, such as the airline industry, government history in bailing out companies has led to a lack of solution and innovation by the companies in question, and, normally, failure.

3.8 Are There Alternatives?

One of the primary findings during a review of general skilled trade business studies is that the studies and resulting recommendations work under the premise that things should remain the same. However, another view would be to embrace the evolution of the new skilled workforce and come up with solutions that provide a new level of productivity in business. Instead of focusing on task-times, the reduction of budgets while maintaining the same requirements, implementation of new R&M concepts and software while maintaining the old philosophies and traditional maintenance: Eliminate the old model and implement a new model.

The old R&M model is not working. Therefore, radical change is required in order to realize improvements and stronger returns-on-investment than continuing in the present direction.

Following are a number of recommendations that can provide a guideline for change and embracing present and near-future changes:

- ✔ If the decision is made to continue apprenticeships and the need for ready-made skills, industry must work directly with academia. There are existing programs with trade schools and community colleges and manufacturers. The manufacturer offers to provide financial assistance to students who meet specific criteria for the company's skilled trade apprentice requirements while working with academia to develop specific curriculum that meets their requirements. The students are then guaranteed a position with the company upon graduation. If they remained employed with the company for a specific length of time (i.e.: 6 to 24 months), then their school loan is forgiven as a bonus. This solution ensures a workforce that meets company needs, provides a basic workforce need for training, and reduces the company's apprenticeship and retention costs.
- ✔ Embrace the changes required to apply EAM/CMMS and ERP within the organization. Applying these technologies to defective systems will only make the weaknesses and problems within the organization appear that much quicker. Instead, select software technologies that meet the corporate needs and apply the reengineering requirements that go with the technology. From the EAM/CMMS perspective,

changes such as the application of CBM should be performed concurrent with the implementation of the software. Recordkeeping, scheduling and work orders should be performed in relation to the software requirements.

✔ Condition-Based Maintenance programs, such as Reliability-Centered Maintenance (RCM), which meet recognized standards (i.e.: SAE JA1011) must be applied. Once applied, the old program, if any, should be eliminated. This avoids the duplication of maintenance tasks and instills a maintenance process. Along with the RCM process, should be a periodic Maintenance Effectiveness Review (MER), which is a continuous improvement process for RCM. The proven impact of properly applied RCM processes will have a significant impact on maintenance costs and overall system reliability and safety.

✔ Condition Monitoring Systems, both route-based and permanently installed, should be investigated for application. Imagine a system that detects an impending problem, alerts the operator and maintenance anywhere, schedules its own corrective maintenance and parts while, in redundant systems, routes around the failed, or failing, part. A dream for the future? No. Such concepts and technologies have been developed and some are ready for commercial application, others are in development and should be available in the near future. Many of these systems utilize WiFi and Bluetooth technology.

✔ Capture the knowledge of veteran skilled workers. Select the best practices and develop both company best practices and procedures. When possible, compare them to industry best practices and procedures to ensure that work has been performed correctly.

✔ Software and Web-Enabled systems for skills and training assessments for the skilled trades exist. Some of these systems include question and answer as well as practical tests. They can be set up to identify both third party and internal training available. This type of approach will dramatically save in training costs and will be more effective by applying the right training to the right person at the right time and for the right reasons.

✔ Include an R&M representative in executive decisions and budgeting efforts. This will ensure that appropriate measures and decisions are made concerning R&M budgeting so that such decisions do not have a negative short or long-term impact on reliability.

✔ Establish clear lines of communication between R&M and management, especially where condition-based decisions must be made.

✔ Develop new and corrective maintenance specifications and procedures with R&M in mind. New equipment should include test points for CBM technologies and inspections as well as technical information to be used for analysis (i.e.: rotor bars, stator slots, bearings, etc). Corrective maintenance specifications must include the gathering of technical information in reports (as with new equipment) and outline expectations. In both cases, ensure that such processes as commissioning for acceptance will be performed, with what technologies and what the pass/fail criteria will be to eliminate surprises and warranty-related arguments.

✔ Develop Commissioning Processes for new and used equipment. In order to ensure that equipment meets your requirements, set commissioning processes to verify that equipment meets specifications.

✔ Develop a 'crash team' of specialists who will make up the core of subject matter experts in order to act as an immediate response and triage team.

✔ Develop an outsourcing process for both specialized and flexible work force. Where it does not make economic sense to maintain technicians for highly specialized diagnosis, maintenance and repair, set up support contracts with vendors tied to response related to criticality of equipment. Additionally, other skills requirements for infrequent or flexible work conditions (i.e.: variable markets that involve frequent layoffs) should have this portion of the workforce outsourced with contracts that allow flexibility. How this is set up and the makeup of the contracted workforce is dependent upon the requirements of the company and the requirements of the contractor. These concepts will allow for flexibility and the ability to lean the workforce based upon the needs of the company without laying off key internal personnel. In some cases, it may be effective to outsource complete basic maintenance, such as the type of programs performed by commercial building services. Qualifications of the workers provided by the contractor must be outlined and the focus should be on best value, not lowest cost.

✔ Embrace technology. There is a significant technology gap between many of the baby boom skilled workforce, in some cases there is significant resistance. This type of situation should be addressed as the company sees appropriate. We understand that this is not a popular concept. However, a workforce that resists technologies that will make the company more effective, equipment available and the workforce more efficient is actually harming the success and, possibly, the survival of the company.

✔ Retain critical employees with value-based incentives.

✔ Utilize vendors as resource partners.

✔ Eliminate task-based maintenance and focus on process-based maintenance.

✔ An understanding by management that a program based upon these, and additional innovative concepts, will result in some portion of the skilled workforce 'waiting' for equipment to fail. One of the key failures in any maintenance program is 'maintenance entropy.' This occurs when a maintenance program becomes successful and the rate of failures and new return on investment opportunities are virtually eliminated. Presently, it is the habit of executives to cut the maintenance budget of a successful program. It is documented that the gap to a reduction in reliability, following the return to a traditional or reactive maintenance program, is 12 to 18 months.

There are other opportunities available perhaps more innovative than those outlined above. These should be considered based upon the environment. Understand that your future maintenance department does NOT have to look like the present.

3.9 Summary

The purpose of this chapter is to provide information and not solutions, a subject for future books. There is, clearly, a difference in opinion between US Federal Government opinion of the US workforce, in particular the skilled maintenance and repair trades, and State Commerce departments and manufacturing. The general appearance is that the Federal agencies are of the opinion that manpower and training, alone, provides the replacement workforce, and not work ethic and experience that manufacturing and maintenance skilled trades require.

The primary concern is that the existing baby-boom workforce is aging and a new generation of workers is reluctant to join. While the skilled trade workforce is expected to decrease with the reduction of manufacturing within the USA, very little new blood is expected to join with an expected reduction in the 16 to 24 year generation of over 1% as a growing number pursue higher education while that population decreases through 2014.

As a result of the progression of the aging workforce, at a rate much higher than the reduction of manufacturing in the USA, and the movement of manufacturing overseas, an industrial crisis is developing within the 2015 to 2020 timeframe, possibly sooner, with the concurrent increase of early retirement offers. The second wave of workers, resulting from the baby-boom-echo generation, will have fewer mentoring opportunities from the aged workforce.

In summary, US manufacturing dominance can be expected to lose ground as a result of overseas competition, the movement of the US manufacturing base overseas, and, most importantly, the loss of the skilled trade infrastructure, within the next 10 to 15 years. A greater gap between an upper class, professional workforce and a lower class, service workforce can also be expected.

Chapter 4

The Relationship of R&M to Corporate Productivity and Profitability

Maintaining the physical assets of a company can have a profound effect on the productivity and profitability of that company. In this chapter, we will cite several real-life examples of the effects of poor maintenance on companies. However, as the companies, themselves, shall remain nameless, the incidences are similar to other issues that we have observed in numerous companies large and small. We will then discuss how to relate successful R&M programs to business success.

4.1 A Case of Poor R&M Practices: Food Processor

Early in 2007, several students at a small middle school in Connecticut felt sick to their stomachs following lunch. In the past, the issue would be investigated through the food service department and the problem dealt with in an appropriate manner. However, things were a little different. There had been a number of scares of sickness and death related to food poisoning at several chain restaurants that had been traced back to poor food processing issues in fresh produce. The nurse determined that the one common element between the students was the milk they had purchased. Instead of following the normal procedure, she contacted the school principle who then contacted the town manager. The town manager initiated the regional anti-terrorism program as it related to poisoning of schoolchildren and called a press conference. The alert required all schools, including private and universities, to pull their milk off the shelf immediately, which they did within hours. [In an interesting note, the food service personnel at the schools in the affected town were not aware of the milk ban until they saw the press conference on TV that evening. The town officials were in such a hurry to have the news conference that they neglected to inform their own schools to pull the milk!]

If the original process had been followed, once the nurse had informed the food service department of the issue, they would have been able to go back through their traceable records in order to determine what and who were affected. They would have then contacted the milk company who would have immediately tested and identified the problem, the associated batches and what needed to be done, as had been accomplished when this instance had occurred in the past. However, the anti-terrorism program required that all the milk be segregated and the company not be allowed to test it. As there was no process for where the milk was to be tested, the six students that had complained had their stomachs pumped. In the meantime, the company started its own investigation and discovered that a maintenance procedure had not been properly followed and that the occurrence had happened a number of times in the past, but the drive to complete the maintenance task by operations was such that short cuts would be taken. The process involved the flushing of piping with a food-grade cleaner between product runs. So, if the company was running white milk and then they were going to package chocolate milk, the food-grade cleaner would be used to flush the lines. There was then the requirement to run product through the lines to remove any remaining cleaner, which was then considered waste, before running the next batch.

As part of the overall program that was launched, the food processor was off-line, being unable to legally manufacture product, until the police force from the small town approved of their processes, even though there were no trained food processing professionals within the force. Therefore, the company was out of business for several days for the entire Northeastern region.

In the meantime, the situation drove the sensitivity of the issue up and alternate drink manufacturers, which were not allowed to include soft drink manufacturers due to other state laws, were put in the position of having to produce enough drink for the region. In fact, the entire process was nearly repeated for a juice processor when the same town manager had required one of the cafeterias to sell orange juice that had been sitting on the dock for several days waiting for the distributor to take it when she had mistook the id code as a date code.

The break down in processes at all levels were hailed as a great victory for the town's anti-terrorism program. In the meantime, the results were customer inconvenience, over-treatment of several children and loss of product sales and reputation through the region. There have been no reported values of the business lost and impact to future sales and reputation from a short cut taken on cleaning process piping.

4.2 A Case of Poor R&M Practices: A Steel Story

A large steel manufacturer for the automotive industry had a robust and well thought out maintenance program, including a condition-based maintenance program that involved the use of outsourced resources over planned shutdowns. Their product was delivered on-time, met customer quality control requirements and relative production costs were substantially lower which more than made up for a slightly higher than normal maintenance budget.

During one of the planned maintenance weekends, one of the reliability contractors called me on a diagnostic question. He said that they had been asked to return to their hotels for the next 48 hours as they ramped up production in order to meet an emergency order from two large automotive companies. As it turns out, he reported, the reason had nothing to do with the particular location, but one of the company's smaller plants in another state.

The other plant manager had made the decision to cut costs by reducing the maintenance budget significantly. At first, production levels and quality remained unchanged and costs did drop. However, within the next few years, in order to maintain production levels, the tolerances on the final product shipped were changed so that the material would pass through Quality Control. The decision to change the tolerances were made internally and not communicated to the customers who, fortunately, did check the tolerances to their specification upon receipt. In one day, a whole week's worth of production was rejected and returned to the plant with the instructions to have another facility produce the material and that the particular facility was never to produce material for them again.

In the end, the properly maintained facility had to cancel some of their maintenance practices, an additional burden was put on machines, the improperly maintained facility lost its customers and the reputation of the company was impacted. The customers, who relied upon Just-in-Time manufacturing processes, were put in a tight spot, including product deliveries. Time, effort, expended energy, customers, reputation and more were damaged or lost due to decisions on getting around the effects of poor maintenance practices.

4.3 A Case of Poor R&M Practices: Another Steel Mill

A large ID fan motor failed on a furnace. The results were over two turns of lost production and all that entails as far as late deliveries, lost production, scrap, etc. An investigative team was sent in to review the cause of failure, which related to blown bearing seals and oil in the motor, poor original manufacture of the motor, broken stator welds and a bad winding. As there were seven other similar motors with the same potential impact, a plan was developed to assist in mitigating the failure.

One month later, the exact same failure pattern occurred on a second motor and the recommendations were repeated. Less than one month later and another motor failed for the same reasons, again. In each case, it was a conscious decision to ignore the findings and recommendations for two basic reasons: no decision is better than a decision; and, what were the chances that the failure would happen again.

On a fourth motor, we were asked to evaluate the condition of a spare, per the maintenance process, before it was installed. By the time we took the data and got back to the maintenance building, the motor had been put in place. Our test results indicated an immediate and severe problem, which we communicated. However, as the commissioning process was bypassed in an effort to save time, the motor was installed and started by the time the installers received word. The motor ran for less than ten seconds before the drive end bearing catastrophically failed. Total lost time—6 turns of production as it also turned out that the motor that was replaced had not failed and was in good condition. The decision to replace it was made solely on the past failures instead of a proper condition assessment.

4.4   A Case of Poor Maintenance Practices: One More Steel Mill

There are large grinders at a particular rolling mill. The purpose of the grinding machines is to grind the surface of the rolls to a high precision so that they can be used to flatten steel from many inches thick to fractions of an inch. You can often see these rolls on the back of flatbed trucks on the highways throughout the country. One of the key issues is 'chatter' on the rolls which would cause defects on the steel as it passes through them. Chatter relates to a non-uniform surface that results from the grinding wheel bouncing on the roll. Operators are paid and rewarded by how many non-defective rolls are ground in a given period.

One of the grinders at this particular location would generate a significant amount of chatter in a pattern that suggested, and was confirmed with vibration analysis, to be at the supply voltage frequency. The grinder manufacturer was brought in and they replaced some parts and left with the equipment in the same condition. It was decided that since the manufacturer was unable to fix the problem that they would have to live with it.

Eighteen months after the problem was identified and the machine was limited to less than half-speed, we reviewed the situation. Using the appropriate condition-based testing technology, we were able to determine, in about 20 minutes, that the cause was a loose connection in the firing circuit of the motor drive. Using a small screwdriver, the loose connection was repaired and the grinder returned to full service.

The lack of the proper technology and the feeling that the manufacturer always understands problems with their equipment led to this issue. Proper training and selection of personnel for troubleshooting these issues is important. The interesting side-note of this story is that one of the electricians had used an oscilloscope and had identified the very problem before the vendor was brought in. His findings were ignored because his managers felt that the vendor should know more than the tradesperson who had been maintaining the equipment since it was installed.

4.5 A Case of Poor Maintenance Practices: Critical Exhaust Fans

In an automotive assembly plant one of the most critical systems is the paint department. This area provides the appearance that is necessary in the sale of a vehicle and is a rather complex process involving air balancing, etc. The supply and exhaust fans used to operate this equipment are critical to the operation and the loss of one motor/fan out of 24 to 36 systems will reduce the ability of the plant to produce significantly.

We were called in to review a motor problem at a 'fan farm' (exhaust fans) relating to electric motor efficiency. As the story went, the vendor was asked to provide a premium efficient electric motor to replace a very old motor, which should have generated an energy cost improvement. The first thing we noticed was that the motor was not what was advertised. Instead, it had a lower efficiency than the original motor, which meant that it cost more to operate than the original. While confirming this with a condition-based technology, we also identified that there were severe problems with the belts in relation to tension, alignment and that the pulley was almost the same size as the motor.

When we continued inquiring about the particular application, we discovered that there was a 40% failure rate of bearings in both the fans and motors. A significant amount of investigation continued and it was determined that this had been continuing for 35 years. We brought in the engineers from a belt manufacturer and worked with them for several months on a solution, which would reduce the failure rate 6% immediately, and lower on motors and fans with replaced bearings.

However, at the beginning of the investigation, when we interviewed the motor repair company, their representative told us point blank that they would prevent any fixes to this particular problem as it was a significant revenue stream for them. They accomplished this by generating fear in the paint department manager that if he were to follow the recommendations that he would look bad and be fired. As the best decision always seems to be 'no decision,' in the realm of many middle managers when it relates to R&M, the manager took the direction of 'no decision.'

4.6 A Case of Poor Maintenance Practices: Welding Transformers

While working for a test instrument manufacturer I received a call concerning the ability of the technology to detect frequent electrical failures in welding transformers. The way the question was brought up prompted a few questions and a discussion related to why the transformers were failing an average of 30-60 days of operation. In this type of application, production welding transformers should last an average of a decade of heavy use.

This type of repetitive failure, in which the Mean Time Between Failure (MTBF), or average time before a piece of equipment fails, is very frequent, usually calls for a technique called Repetitive Failure Analysis (RFA). In almost every case, instead of analyzing and fixing the problem a company will look at better ways to detect the early failure resulting in an acceptance of less than ideal conditions that have a major impact on the business. Sometimes these types of issues actually generate their own place in the maintenance budget.

In this particular case, it was determined that the wrong transformer was selected in the design process. The company engineers selected a proper grade of transformer and the failure rate all but disappeared.

4.7 Don't Read This If You Are On An Airplane

In 2006, I traveled round trip on aircraft over 43 weeks. As I write an R&M eNewsletter, I pay specific attention to maintenance-related concerns and had at least one airline related significant comment at least every 2-3 weeks. These issues included such issues as waterline breaks to the coffee pot that were not repaired because it would require 2-3 days of repair and the water was leaking into a battery compartment to all of the bathrooms not working on an aircraft to the inability to land at one airport because the instrumentation that would have allowed them to land in a light fog was inoperable.

While most of the issues were amusing, a few occurred in 2007 that were downright disturbing and one of the reasons for this section. The issues outline the impact of some of the actions that are taking place in many facilities which, luckily, only impact productivity, throughput and profitability as well as some safety.

Several particular issues in 2006 and 2007 included:

- On a return flight following a conference, the pilot and ground crew had finished their walk around the aircraft and the door was closed. A passenger in the window seat beside me contacted the stewardess to report fluid pouring out of the right engine. It was identified as a failed hydraulic line and we were removed from the aircraft and transferred, as standby, on other aircraft.
- I was sitting next to a tradesman in the last seat of an aircraft flying out to Detroit from Connecticut. While we were talking about some of the R&M issues within his facility (I serve on a UAW and management joint task team for maintenance best practices for one of the big three) we were both repeatedly having to put the tray back in place from the empty seat between us. I said, 'if their maintenance issues on this aircraft are this obvious, what else is wrong?' Apparently, a cracked windshield and failed APU (an item used to self-start the engines and run the air conditioning referred to as an Auxiliary Power Unit). We were put on another aircraft.

- The tray table for a woman sitting across from me had the tab missing that holds the tray in place. A mechanic came on board and wound duct tape around the back of the chair to hold the tray in place and informed the woman that she would be unable to use the tray table. He filled out paperwork that stated that the problem was fixed (I looked over his shoulder), had the captain sign it and left the aircraft.
- I was writing one of my newsletters on another aircraft. I write my drafts using pen and paper. The stewardess and captain asked me what I was writing and I said that I write a maintenance newsletter. Just before the doors closed the captain comes back out and identifies that they have a cracked windshield, a problem with his chair and the APU failed. They asked me not to write anything about the incident, which I did in the very newsletter I was drafting.
- I was upgraded to first class on another flight. Before takeoff I asked for a cup of coffee and the stewardess let me know that there would be no coffee because of a leaky waterline. This had been a problem for days, so I asked why they had not taken care of it. The reason I was given by the stewardess was that it would take several days because the leak was located directly above a battery bank. Unlike the past, the airline was lean on available aircraft so was required to 'live with' this situation for some time. I had no complaints as the stewardess had brought on a thermos and shared some of her coffee with me.
- There were many, many more delays, cancelled flights and other issues related to maintenance in just the 70 plus flights I took on multiple air carriers in 2006.

In 2007, two incidences helped change how I viewed travel. Mind you that I continue to fly on a regular basis, just less than in the past.

- The first incident was related to a flight from Connecticut to Detroit on one of my frequent airlines. It was my usual 9am flight on the Monday of the week I spent with my big three client and very routine, other than we had an important meeting that afternoon. The aircraft was started and the door closed. A few seconds later the captain walked briskly down the aisle to the back of the aircraft holding a flashlight then back to the front a few minutes later then back again with a contract maintenance mechanic. We were then informed by the frustrated captain that we would have to de-plane and be rescheduled on other flights. When I asked one of the aircrew what had happened, I was informed that the aircraft had gone through a maintenance inspection over the weekend in which the gaskets for the emergency doors were inspected. The rear of the DC-10 is an emergency 'cone' that can be removed as an emergency door. When the aircraft was pressurized, the alarm went off that told the captain that they could not maintain pressure in the aircraft and he discovered that the cone was not attached properly. The crewperson informed me that, "If the maintenance had not been performed incorrectly, and the gasket had not been worn out, we would not have known the back end was not fastened properly until we hit altitude." The remainder of the story relates to how it took four hours to obtain my luggage as they were not able to place me on another flight until Wednesday of that week so I had to drive the 9.5 hours to Detroit that evening. Of particular interest was that during my research for a part of this section on the US Department of Transportation's Inspector General's website was a report entitled, "Actions Taken To Address Allegations of Unsafe Maintenance Practices at Northwest Airlines," FAA Report Number AV-2007-080 issued September 28, 2007, where they discuss some of the issues that led up to this kind of problem.

- Even more disturbing was the flight the very next week on a different airline. I was taking a trip to Chicago from Connecticut and was in the middle of drafting my article concerning my experiences the week before. I heard but was not really paying too much attention to several calls for the steward on my side of the aircraft. The doors were already closed and we were backing away from the gate when the captain came on and stated, "Don't mind the missing inspection hatch on the left engine, it does not impact the airworthiness of the aircraft." I stated, "But if something that obvious is missing, what else is wrong?" At which point I was told by a member of the aircrew that I was causing a disturbance and would be removed and arrested if I said another word.

One of the items of particular interest about this section is that the aircraft industry has been outsourcing maintenance both domestically and abroad at a significant rate. I was aware of this, and had been actively participating in discussions related to this issue, but did not become seriously concerned until I read some of the reports related to the issue while writing this book.

The Inspector General's office studied six US airlines, which are not named in the report. It found that none were providing an adequate level of [maintenance] training. One airline provided 11 hours of classroom and video training while another simply provided a one hour video. One airline simply mailed a workbook to each shop and required mechanics to sign a form saying they had read it.

JetBlue, Southwest, America West, Northwest and United are among the carriers who outsource major maintenance of their aircraft in other countries, The Wall Street Journal reported earlier.

To provide a broader overview, the Inspector General reviewed 19 airlines and found that one of them outsourced just 1 percent of its total maintenance while another outsourced 39 percent. At one unnamed airline, noncertified contractors performed 74 percent of critical repairs, those that require an inspection before the airplane goes back into service.[14]

---

[14] ConsumerAffairs.com, *Airline Maintenance Questioned: Outsourcing Critical Repairs Already Blamed for One Fatal Crash,* December 27, 2005

This article follows a January 22, 2005 article by the same source:

Their business plans differ in many ways, but there's one area where major airlines and their cut-rate competitors agree: maintenance is a lot cheaper when it's performed by lower-paid mechanics working for outsourcers.

JetBlue, Southwest, America West, Northwest and United are among the carriers who outsource major maintenance of their aircraft to contractors in other countries, according to a report in The Wall Street Journal.

- *As JetBlue's new A320 Airbus fleet ages, aircraft are sent to a repair hub in El Salvador;*
- *America West also sends its jets to El Salvador;*
- *Southwest has always outsourced its major maintenance;*
- *US Airways mechanics agreed Friday to pay cuts and the outsourcing of 2,000 mechanics jobs;*
- *Northwest sends its wide-body jets to Singapore and Hong Kong;*
- *Bankrupt United Airlines recently won union approval to begin using outside contractors for heavy maintenance.*

It wasn't long ago that major airlines employed their own highly-skilled mechanics each with his or her own Federal Aviation Administration license. The mechanics, who often studied for two years before taking the test, could make $60 or more per hour.

Mechanics working for outsourcers don't have to be licensed. Only supervisors are required to hold FAA licenses and are responsible for oversight of the mechanics, who in countries like El Salvador may make $10 to $20 per hour.

Is this endangering long-term safety of the US commercial fleet? The airlines say no but others aren't sure.

Last year, investigators found that deficient maintenance by an outside vendor was partly to blame for the 2003 crash of a commuter flight in Charlotte, NC that killed 21 people.

In 1999, ValuJet Flight 592 crashed into the Florida Everglades after taking off from Miami International Airport, killing all 110 on board. The crash was attributed to oxygen

*canisters improperly stowed in the aircraft's hold by mainte-
nance employees working for an outside contractor.*

*American Airlines says it prefers to keep heavy mainte-
nance in-house because it has a well-trained, highly seasoned
workforce. It outsources only 20% of its maintenance and
none of its heavy tear-downs.*[15]

I do have to note here that American Airlines was the only airline
where I did not have maintenance related stories to write about.

Now, why does this have particular interest for our industrial
and manufacturing facilities? And, why does this topic fit into this
particular chapter?

With maintenance viewed as a cost-cutting opportunity by management, outsourcing maintenance and advanced maintenance
practices, such as condition-based maintenance and predictive
maintenance, has become an increasing option. However, with the
cost reduction, is the company truly receiving cost benefits or other
improvements? Or, is the company reducing the perceived cost of
maintaining equipment while surrendering a significant productivity and profit opportunity through proper investment in asset maintenance management?

Well, let's explore this a little further by actually taking a peek
inside the findings and conclusions of the report "Air Carriers' Use
of Non-Certificated Repair Facilities."[16]

*The contract maintenance that most people are familiar
with and that we have previously reported on involves aircraft repair facilities that are certificated by FAA. FAA has evaluated these facilities to verify that they have the staff and
equipment needed to complete the type of maintenance work
the facility is approved to perform. However, there is another
segment of the repair industry that is widely used by air carriers but is neither certificated nor routinely reviewed by FAA:
non-certificated repair facilities.*

---

[15] ConsumerAffairs.com, *Airlines Outsourcing More Maintenance,* January 22, 2005
[16] US Department of Transportation, *Air Carriers' Use of Non-Certificated Repair Facilities,* Report Number AV-2006-031, December 15, 2005

Air carriers have used non-certificated facilities for years, but it was widely accepted that these facilities were principally used to perform minor maintenance tasks, and only performed more significant work in emergency situations. However, our review determined that this is not the case today—we identified 6 domestic and foreign facilities that performed scheduled maintenance, and 21 that performed maintenance critical to the airworthiness of the aircraft. FAA permits use of these facilities as long as the work is approved by an FAA-certificated mechanic.

The importance of effective oversight of non-certificated repair facilities became evident in the aftermath of the January 2003 Air Midwest crash in Charlotte, North Carolina. Independent contract mechanics, certificated by FAA and working for a non-certificated company, completed maintenance on the aircraft the day before the accident. The mechanics incorrectly adjusted a flight control system that ultimately was determined to be a contributing cause of the crash—this work was also approved by an FAA-certificated mechanic employed by the non-certificated company. The National Transportation Safety Board determined that contributing causes of the accident included Air Midwest's lack of oversight of the work performed by mechanics working for the non-certificated entity and lack of FAA oversight of Air Midwest's maintenance program.

Major carriers spend up to $4.9 billion annually for aircraft maintenance. Currently, over 50 percent of this maintenance is performed by external repair facilities. Based on our review, a substantial majority of these facilities are certificated by FAA. But non-certificated repair facilities are now performing more significant work than anyone realized.[17]

What are some of the differences between the certificated repair facilities and the less expensive non-certificated repair facilities?

---

[17] US Department of Transportation, *Air Carriers' Use of Non-Certificated Repair Facilities,* Report Number AV-2006-031, December 15, 2005

There are key regulatory differences in the operation of a certificated repair station and a non-certificated repair entity. FAA performs inspections of FAA-certificated repair stations to ensure they maintain detailed records on the work performed; have the appropriate equipment, housing and staff to perform the work; and have a quality control system to ensure work is performed properly. In contrast, inspections of non-certificated facilities are not covered as part of FAA's routine oversight program. In other words, requirements that come with obtaining an FAA repair station certificate provide an additional layer of controls that are lacking at non-certificated facilities.[18]

As part of our review of air carrier maintenance records, we identified 20 additional non-certificated facilities performing critical maintenance work, such as repairs to parts used to measure airspeed and repairs to aircraft doors. Other examples of work we identified that non-certificated facilities perform include:

- *On-call maintenance:*
  - *Replacing aircraft tires*
  - *Resetting circuit breakers*
  - *Servicing engine fluids*
- *Scheduled maintenance:*
  - *Detailed interior and exterior checks that verify the airworthiness of the aircraft*
  - *Daily checks to evaluate wings, engine, landing gear, and flight control systems for damage*
  - *Inspections of crew and passenger oxygen, aircraft fuselage, wings, and engines for discrepancies at prescribed time intervals*
  - *Repairs to hydraulic valves required by FAA Airworthiness Directives*
- *Critical aircraft repairs:*
  - *Removing and replacing an engine*

---

[18] US Department of Transportation, *Air Carriers' Use of Non-Certificated Repair Facilities*, Report Number AV-2006-031, December 15, 2005

○ *Replacing flight control motors*

○ *Removing and replacing aircraft doors[19]*

Of particular concern is the lack of oversight of the non-certificated facilities.

While FAA relies upon air carrier training and oversight programs, we found significant shortcomings in all six air carrier programs we reviewed. Examples of these shortcomings follow.

• *Training of mechanics ranged from 1-hour video to 11 hours of combined video and classroom training. One US air carrier mailed a workbook to each non-certificated facility and told mechanics to read the information and fax back a signed form indicating they had completed the carrier's training. Conversely, some foreign air carriers require mechanics to have 2 months of training before they can work on the carrier's aircraft. The training air carriers provided to mechanics at non-certified facilities before they complete critical repairs was particularly problematic. FAA requires that mechanics performing critical repairs receive specialized training on those repairs. However, we found that mechanics at non-certificated repair facilities were not receiving detailed training on this type of maintenance work. Typically, air carriers only provided mechanics at non-certificated facilities with telephone briefings to perform this maintenance.*

• *Air carrier oversight of non-certificated facilities was limited. One of the six air carriers we reviewed performed no oversight of its non-certificated facilities. The other five air carriers did perform evaluations of the facility operations (e.g., reviewed tool calibration and fulfillment of air carrier training) but did not review the actual maintenance work the facilities performed to ensure they met air carrier requirements. One air carrier used a 2-page checklist of superficial questions requiring a 'yes' or 'no' response as its*

---

[19] US Department of Transportation, *Air Carriers' Use of Non-Certificated Repair Facilities*, Report Number AV-2006-031, December 15, 2005

audit of the facility's work. For example, one question on the checklist was 'does the vendor have a fax machine?'

According to FAA officials, when an FAA certificated mechanic performs work for an air carrier, the mechanic does so under the quality system of the air carrier and becomes an extension of the air carrier's maintenance organization. While this may be true, the air carrier quality systems we reviewed could be improved, specifically with respect to the training air carriers provided mechanics at non-certificated facilities and the oversight provided of the work they performed. Our concerns were reinforced by examples of discrepancies we identified when we reviewed maintenance records for 6 air carriers and 10 repair facilities. These discrepancies included cases of improper maintenance procedures, overlooked maintenance discrepancies, and incorrect logbook entries. For instance, our review of one air carrier's maintenance records disclosed a non-certified facility that overlooked at least five major maintenance discrepancies (e.g., burn marks on a flight control system) while performing a lightning strike inspection.[20]

We also identified non-certificated facilities that performed repairs that were so important to overall airworthiness of the aircraft that FAA requires a special inspection to be performed on the aircraft once the repairs are completed. Some examples of this work include:

- *14 of the 19 (74 percent) critical repairs (i.e., performed with a one-time required inspection item authorization) performed for an air carrier during a 3-year period were done by non-certificated repair facilities. Examples of the work performed include landing gear checks, lightning strike inspections and door slide replacements.*
- *16 of the 45 (36 percent) critical repairs performed for another air carrier from March 2003 to October 2004 were done by non-certificated repair facilities. Examples of this work included removing and replacing parts used for*

---

[20] US Department of Transportation, *Air Carriers' Use of Non-Certificated Repair Facilities,* Report Number AV-2006-031, December 15, 2005

Table 3: Examples of Differences in Requirements for Certificated and Non-Certificated Facilities

FAA Requirements	Certificated Repair Station	Non-Certificated Repair Station
Quality Control System	Required	Not Required
Designated Supervisors and Inspectors	Required	Not Required
Training Program	Required	Not Required

Table 4: Differences in Requirements for Certified and Non-Certified Maintenance Facilities

Requirement	Certified Repair Station	Non-Certified Repair Station
FAA Inspections	Annual Inspection Required	No Requirement
Quality Control System	Must establish and maintain a quality control system that ensures that repairs performed by the facility or subcontractor are in compliance with regulations	No Requirement
Reporting Failures, Malfunctions and Defects	Must report failures, malfunctions and defects to FAA within 96 hours of discovery	No Requirement
Personnel	Must have designated supervisors, inspectors and return-to-service personnel	No Requirement
Training Program	Required	No Requirement
Facilities and Housing	If authorized to perform airframe repairs, must have facilities large enough to house the aircraft they are authorized to repair	No Requirement

Table 5: Examples of Logbook Errors by Non-Certificated Repair Facilities

Logbook Discrepancy	Improper Action Taken by Mechanic	Significance of Event
Improper representation of the work performed	Logbook page incorrectly stated that a repair was performed when it had actually been deferred.	The improper logbook entry meant the pilot did not know that the aircraft had a malfunctioning aircraft control system
Failure to enter discrepancy identified or corrective action taken	Inspected forward cargo door seal but never entered the discrepancy or the outcome of the inspection into the logbook	The aircraft logbook did not fully represent all maintenance and inspections performed on the aircraft, which are important for trend analysis of repetitive problems.
Proper maintenance procedures were not entered in logbook	Reset a tripped fuel boost-pump circuit breaker without following proper procedures or entering proper procedures in logbook	Performing this repair without following the proper procedures would cause a fire or fuel tank explosion.

flight controls, parts used to measure airspeed, and air-craft doors.

- *One non-certificated facility completed maintenance tasks required by an Airworthiness Directive on three aircraft operated by a US air carrier. The carrier had advance notice of this maintenance requirement but still elected to use a non-certificated facility to complete the work. The maintenance work was required to prevent failure of the hydraulic shut-off valve, which could have resulted in leakage of hydraulic fluid into the engine fire zone, a reduced ability to*

retract landing gear, a loss of backup electrical power, and
consequently the reduced controllability of the aircraft.[21]

The thought process of saving or reducing labor costs through outsourcing maintenance can have both a positive and negative impact. While the direct maintenance budget may appear to decrease, due to reduced direct maintenance labor costs, it is likely that opportunities that a company can control through direct qualification of personnel may be lost. These are the indirect maintenance improvements that impact cost, reputation, and more.

For instance, with the ValuJet Florida crash, who remembers the subcontractor who performed the work that contributed to the accident? The reputation of the company is as good as its least reliable contractor.

Later in this book we will cover concepts for the proper timing and selection of contract maintenance and how to avoid some of the common pitfalls. Such organizations can provide an outstanding resource, assuming they are qualified to perform the work.

4.8 The Impact of a Properly Implemented R&M Program

The following graphics depict the overall cost improvements to a large steel manufacturer through the successful implementation of a full R&M program. The success required the full support of executive management, middle management and the plant floor.

The success of this program did require some upfront investment in a program called Reliability-Centered Maintenance (RCM). The objective was to first determine what equipment should be focused on and then determine which improvements will bring immediate results.

By identifying what maintenance should be performed, the company was also able to identify personnel improvements that were implemented through voluntary attrition (Figure 8).

---

[21] US Department of Transportation, *Air Carriers' Use of Non-Certificated Repair Facilities,* Report Number AV-2006-031, December 15, 2005

Figure 5: Proactive Maintenance Improvement from Reliability Program

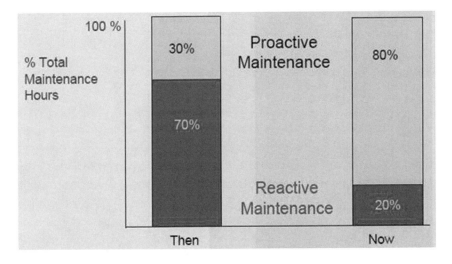

Figure 6: Equipment Availability Improvements

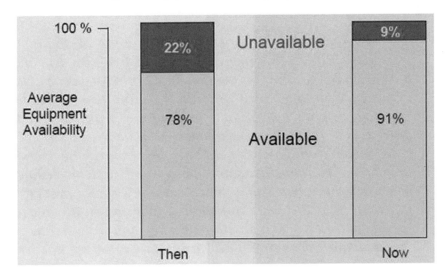

Figure 7: End Product Quality Improvements

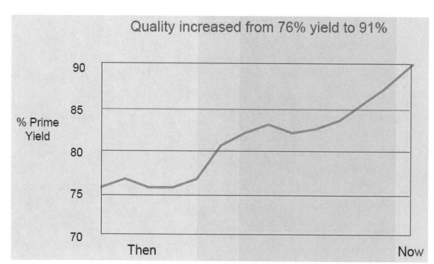

Quality increased from 76% yield to 91%

All of this was performed while production increased. Within a decade, the steel company went from being an average steel company to the most profitable steel manufacturer in North America.

The advantages of predictive maintenance are many. A well-orchestrated predictive maintenance program will all but eliminate catastrophic equipment failures. We will be able to schedule maintenance activities to minimize or delete overtime cost. We will be able to minimize inventory and order parts, as required, well ahead of time to support the downstream maintenance needs. We can optimize the operation of the equipment, saving energy cost and increasing plant reliability. Past studies have estimated that a properly functioning predictive maintenance program can provide a savings of 8-12% over a program utilizing preventive maintenance alone. Depending on a facility's reliance on reactive maintenance and material condition, it could easily recognize savings opportunities exceeding 30-40%. In fact, independent surveys indicate the following industrial average savings resultant from initiation of a functional predictive maintenance program:

Figure 8: Manpower Changes

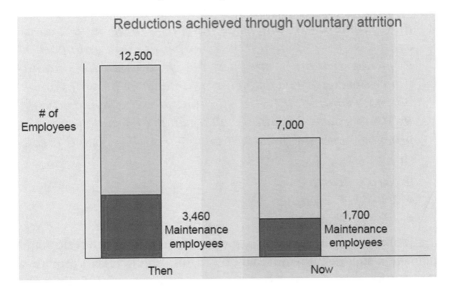

- *Return on investment: 10 times*
- *Reduction in maintenance costs: 25-30%*
- *Elimination of breakdowns: 70-75%*
- *Reduction in downtime: 35-45%*
- *Increase in production: 20-25%[22]*

Basically, RCM methodology deals with some key issues not dealt with by other maintenance programs. It recognizes that all equipment in a facility is not of equal importance to either the process or facility safety. It recognizes that equipment design and operation differs and that different equipment will have a higher probability to undergo failures from different degradation mechanisms than others. It also approaches the structuring of a maintenance program recognizing that a facility does not have unlimited financial and personnel resources and that the use of both need to be prioritized and optimized. In a nutshell, RCM is a systematic approach to evaluate a facility's equipment and resources to

---

[22] Federal Energy Management Program, *Operations & Maintenance Best Practices*, US DOE, 1999

best mate the two and result in a high degree of facility relia-bility and cost-effectiveness. RCM is highly reliant on predictive maintenance but also recognizes that maintenance activities on equipment that is inexpensive and unimportant to facility reliability may best be left to a reactive maintenance approach. The following maintenance program breakdowns of continually top-performing facilities would echo the RCM approach to utilize all available maintenance approaches with the predominant methodology being predictive.

- *<10% Reactive*
- *25-35% Preventive*
- *45-55% Predictive*

From this point, we will begin to discuss how to develop and manage a successful maintenance organization that will provide a significant impact on the success, productivity and profitability of your company.

Chapter 5

Overview of the Successful Development of Maintenance Management

Regardless of the type of maintenance philosophy or best practices that you follow, there are basic steps that are required for any successful maintenance program. In this chapter we will discuss these basic steps. The remainder of the book will discuss how the program can be managed, strategies, structures and the business impact of the overall R&M organization.

Figure 9: Functions of a Successful Program

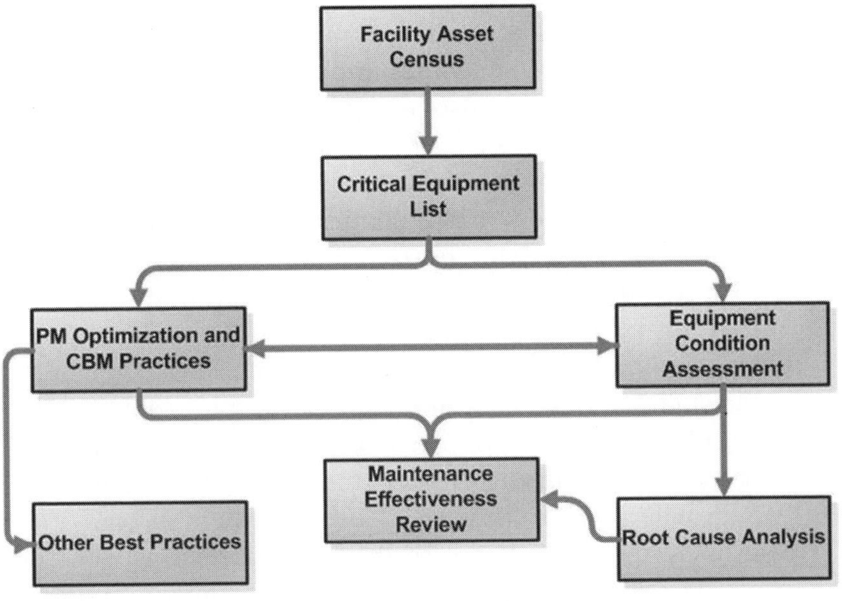

```
              ┌──────────────────┐
              │  Facility Asset  │
              │      Census      │
              └──────────────────┘
                       │
                       ▼
              ┌──────────────────┐
              │ Critical Equipment│
              │       List       │
              └──────────────────┘
```

┌──────────────────┐   ┌──────────────────┐
│ PM Optimization and│◄─────────────────►│   Equipment   │
│   CBM Practices   │   │   Condition   │
└──────────────────┘   │   Assessment   │
                                        └──────────────────┘
              ┌──────────────────┐
              │   Maintenance   │
              │ Effectiveness   │
              │   Review   │
              └──────────────────┘
┌──────────────────┐   ┌──────────────────┐
│Other Best Practices│   │ Root Cause Analysis│
└──────────────────┘   └──────────────────┘

5.1 Facility Asset Census

The Facility Asset Census (FAC) is extremely important to the application of any maintenance program. The purpose is to know what you own before taking the next steps that will assist in determining what resources are necessary to maintain and provide continuous improvement to your program.

Through observations and site visits from small manufacturers to Fortune 100 companies, it has been readily identifiable that most companies do not know what they own or the resources that they have available. In effect, poor asset management is also driven by not understanding what assets exist and their condition and impact on the corporation. These resources include:

- Property: Buildings, land and other real estate. What is the condition? Value? Potential value if updated or maintained? The gap for improvements and associated investments?
- Equipment: Both production-related such as end product or service equipment, including vehicles, and facility-related, such as fire pumps, compressors, fans, air conditioning, electrical distribution, etc.
- People: Operations, skilled and unskilled labor, management, engineering, sales, and other personnel and positions as well as capabilities. This becomes important as the organization comes together as it also assists in determining the investment in training and/or outsourcing different components of the R&M group. What is the potential buy-in of employees, middle management and senior management? Is there a level of understanding that must be employed in order to develop a successful program? Will your people support it and do you have any potential champions?
- Information: Historical information, purchasing information, the ability to obtain the information and the accuracy of the information in paper or digital form. Knowing what information is available in all forms and the accuracy of that information will provide the basis for implementing the R&M strategy, including knowing that the information does not exist. Additional competitive information concerning your in-

dustry and similar industries is also important in order to set mile-markers for your programs.

- Other Resources:This includes vendors and their capabilities, outsourced maintenance capabilities, emergency services and what level of knowledge you maintain concerning those organizations.Are there general industry resources available? Also, what in-house technologies, inspections methods, laboratories and other resources are available?

- Reputation:How do your employees, competitors, vendors and customers view your organization? How would you like them to view your organization? For instance, if your customers have a general inclination towards 'green' organizations, how can you use your R&M group to demonstrate that your company is 'green?' Could it be that you set goals of installing energy efficient or alternative energy systems as older legacy systems fail? Even at a higher cost so that you can market the environmental and energy policies of your organization?

At first this type of effort can be daunting, especially when a majority of your staff managers and labor, alike, will go to great lengths to state that the company already knows this information. Many feel that is an affront to their position that they do not know something, others may actually not fully understand the importance and, let's face it, there are many who just plain do not want to put forth the effort. In any case, in any organization, you will find that a great deal of information is missing in each of these categories. Some of it hidden, some of it obvious.And all of it may not be caught in the initial census, which means that a method of continuous improvement and updating will be required.

Once the information is obtained, the complete organization, systems and inter-relationships can be mapped, which may put a whole different perspective on how the company is managed.

5.2 The Critical Equipment List

As each grouping of systems and their inter-relationships are determined, it then becomes simpler to evaluate the systems in order to develop the Critical Equipment List (CEL).The CEL is used to rank each of the systems and components of the systems in order to identify how much attention that system will require in the maintenance program. This is a significant step in determining what resources will be required, and the skill sets, in order to maintain or improve the physical assets of the organization.

The general categories for critical equipment are as follow:

- Personnel Safety: In virtually all maintenance philosophies, this level of criticality is considered number one. In effect, this category relates to systems that will impact human safety such as fire protection systems, exit lights, ladders, harnesses, equipment guarding, etc.
- Regulatory Issues: This concerns systems that have regulatory impact such as EPA, OSHA, and other regulatory bodies associated with your industry. For instance, this impacts emission controls and what impact they have on your organization.
- Production/Mission: What impact will the systems have on production or mission of the company? This category is often set up in three to ten levels of criticality, depending on what maintenance philosophy you are following. For instance, if it is set up as a three category system, a Category A may impact the entire facility's ability to produce, a Category B may impact individual systems and a Category C may have no impact on production. In any case, these categories, or levels, should reflect the priorities of your company.
- Cost: This reflects the cost to repair or replace a component or system in relation to the cost to maintain it. While many organizations put a general dollar figure on this topic, such as $25,000, in reality there is much more thought that is required. For instance, if the item is worth $5000 and the effort to maintain it is only $50 per year, then it would be cost effective to maintain. The rules to determine this are normally agreed by the maintenance organization or committee and will also include the availability of replacements and repair facility turnaround.
- Other Company Priorities: This is often left out by maintenance organizations, but can be one of the more important categories.

For instance, if an R&M organization is developing the maintenance procedures for an airline and they look at the cleaning staff going on the plane at the end of each leg of a flight, they may ask what impact that has on the reliability, safety, regulations, mission or cost of the airworthiness of the aircraft. The answer, of course, would be 'none.' However, the indirect impact would be customers who would be less inclined to fly that particular airline because of the cleanliness of the aircraft. Yet, this is one of the pitfalls of many of the maintenance philosophies, in the effort to reduce cost and labor related to maintenance, critical factors may be overlooked or eliminated.

The important aspect to the CEL is that this list represents the equipment that must be maintained and to provide the information necessary to determine to what extreme. All other equipment that does not make this list can then be evaluated to determine if it can be run to failure.

5.3 PM Optimization and CBM Practices

Once the critical equipment has been selected, then the effort towards improving the maintenance practices begin. This involves two approaches and must be performed in digestible chunks, or the program will fail.

The first, and necessary, approach is PM Optimization. There are a number of different philosophies behind this, depending on which consultant or book is used to reference. However, they all follow the same basic principles and can have an immediate impact. The first step is to determine which systems are not going to be maintained and will be run to failure. The second step should include the ability to either move the equipment on to the CEL or to remove all of the maintenance associated with the system or component.

The next step involves the implementation of the maintenance philosophy whether that is Reliability-Centered Maintenance (RCM), Total Productive Maintenance (TMP), Total Quality Maintenance (TQM), Six-Sigma, other program or hybrid. As each of these processes is developed and the associated maintenance practices are created for each system, then the old maintenance practices must be removed and the new ones implemented.

In one case, we went to evaluate a facility and we were brought up to observe a condition-based maintenance practice on an air handler. The maintenance staff had placed windows on either side of the filter system and a static pressure gage was set up so that the optimal pressure range was in green, then yellow and finally red to show outside of the range. The maintainer showed us how he looked into the ports, checked the gage and then checked off the item on his work order that the filter was good. We returned to the air handler to observe a remote vibration device that they had attached and noticed that another maintainer was removing and re-placing the large filter that we had seen checked off as good. When queried, the maintainer stated simply that even though the filter was good, they had to meet their maintenance scheduling comple-tion goals and this work order was still cited.

5.4 Equipment Condition Assessment

Both during and after the PM Optimization and CBM Practices de-velopment, the histories and evaluation of the critical equipment as to its condition must be reviewed. In many cases, this point is where the first set of testing is performed and where baselines are set. It should also not come as a surprise that corrective maintenance costs may go up slightly during this phase as one out of four to one out of six pieces of equipment will show defects that should be scheduled for corrective action.

5.5 Root-Cause-Analysis

As with all of the other steps, this one is also a continuous improve-ment initiative. This part of the program is associated with Root-Cause-Failure-Analysis (RCFA), Repetitive Failure Analysis (RFA) and Root-Cause-Analysis (RCA). Each of these processes have slightly different reasons but follow similar steps, depending upon which discipline or hybrid of disciplines you use.

The RCFA is primarily used when a critical piece of equipment fails unexpectedly. It works under the premise that there is some root cause much deeper than just the obvious failure point and immediate chain of events. For instance, with the Florida Everglades crash example of the previous chapter, while the misplacement of oxygen bottles by a non-certificated maintenance organization is the immediate finding, what processes, procedures and other direct and indirect practices allowed the non-certificated maintenance organization perform that task? And, how do you avoid the same issue from happening in the future? Or, is it something that you are willing to risk?

The concept of the Root-Cause-Analysis is to take the RCFA one step further, or before a critical system fails. In the same example above, instead of limiting ourselves to the one system, we would be using RCA to evaluate what other systems may have similar issues. In this case, the concept is to identify root causes before the equipment fails.

The RFA process is also similar. However, the focus is on any systems that are seeing repetitive failures, such as the welding transformer example in the previous chapter. Once it was noticed that failures were happening on a routine basis, an RFA should have been implemented. However, it is often the case that repetitive failures become routine maintenance practices.

The results from these root cause processes are then fed into the key continuous improvement component, the Maintenance Effectiveness Review (MER).

5.6 The Maintenance Effectiveness Review

The MER is an extremely powerful and extremely effective part of the maintenance process that is virtually always forgotten in any R&M program, whether it is in its infancy or mature. This is considered the continuous improvement portion of the program. A properly implemented MER will take in all of the information related to systems within the facility, provide rules to evaluate the effectiveness of the maintenance being performed, eliminate redundancies and continue to lean out the maintenance process.

The key concept to the development of any maintenance program is to remember this one statement, if none other:

**The Purpose of Any R&M Continuous Improvement
Program or Maintenance Development Program is to**

determine what the maintenance budget and process should be, not to meet a specific budget and process.

5.7 Other Best Practices

The concept of developing maintenance best practices is to provide the ground rules for how maintenance is to be performed from a common practice and process standpoint. Unfortunately, many programs rely upon just the individual maintenance technician and not a common practice. This is contrary to the practices that were developed in the 1800's and early 1900's related to production, production improvement and the assembly line.

A written best practice should consist of a scope, justification, procedure and the expected benefits from the application. The procedure is normally very specific and may take some time and research to develop such as understanding the type of work, verifying that the practice that is being developed is, in fact, the best method that can be determined at the time, and that it can be used in order to determine how much time certain functions, such as greasing, alignment, etc. should take, on average.

For instance, a best practice may be developed around greasing electric motor bearings. This is a common and controversial area when considering the maintenance process. In the review we performed for a client, we discovered that there were literally dozens of ways that the greasing process was being performed and that several manufacturers were even developing products to assist the end user in improperly greasing bearings. We were then able to take that process, apply times to each step and that now allows the planning and scheduling people to get their part of the process together.

5.8 The Concept and Principle of Process Maintenance

The military is commonly referred to as the 'uniform services.' The reason is that they commonly perform the same things in pretty much the same ways including dress code, thought process, etc.

One of the primary reasons that the military is so effective at the maintenance process and some of the best maintenance people are former military (especially Navy), is that maintenance is performed via a Maintenance Requirement Card (MRC). On each card is indicated:

- Title of the maintenance
- Responsibility for the maintenance
- Frequency of the maintenance
- Location of the items to be maintained
- A reference to a master schedule
- Who is qualified to perform the maintenance
- The materials that will be required including tools, parts and consumables
- The amount of time the maintenance will take to perform
- A step-by-step process for performing the maintenance
- Any drawings or materials required

The result is a process that allows for simple On-the-Job-Training (OJT), classroom training, reminders to ensure that the maintenance is uniform so that if anything does go wrong it is easier to perform an RCFA or a MER can be set up to be more effective. The steps that go into an MRC are considered the best practices for that particular maintenance. One other key benefit is also introduced: More effective use of maintenance personnel and improved wrench-time.

However, when we set up maintenance in our facilities, the scheduled PM work orders will often just say to 'grease bearings,' without a detailed procedure. The result is that a variety of methods are performed that may be less effective, more time consuming or outright incorrect. Through the development and management of the maintenance program, more control of the program can be exercised through proper process-based maintenance procedures.

Chapter 6

Getting the Maintenance Process Under Control: Planning and Scheduling

In the previous chapters, we have outlined the basics of the physical asset management process. In this chapter, however, we will go into more technical detail as this particular area involves managing, controlling and improving wrenchtime of the maintenance staff. This is of particular importance as the average 'wrench time,' or time performed doing useful work, tends to be in the 20-40% range. This means that per maintenance employee you may only be getting less than 1 to 4 hours per 8 hour shift of useful work. However, this is not a maintenance issue, it is a management issue.

Planning and scheduling tasks tend to be based upon fixed times in both the internal and contracted maintenance arena. This can lead to inefficient or ineffective use of resources and the decline of the maintenance department towards reactive maintenance, further reducing the efficiency of the program. There are a number of ways to not only ensure proper completion of maintenance tasks, both scheduled and reactive, but also to improve wrench time.

In the production and operations arena, there are a number of methods of scheduling production for maximum efficiency. The method for getting the most out of the process is by determining, first, if the production method is a job shop, batch, assembly line or continuous flow. Once operations has determined the type of process, scheduling can be performed using simple methods, with unknowns including suppliers and uptime. In fact, some planning methods review production and take into account reduced throughput due to improper maintenance without realizing it.

Maintenance is slightly different in that it can be a combination of all four systems. For instance:

1. Reactive Maintenance (RM):This is a job-shop process where each repair and return to service is handled on a case-by-case basis.
2. Preventive Maintenance (PM): Depending on the type of PM, this can be job-shop, batch or assembly.
3. Predictive/Condition-Based Maintenance (PdM/CBM):These are generally batch or assembly with continuous monitoring falling under continuous flow.

Add in the variable of individual training, experience and aging of the workforce, planning and scheduling can become quite complex, with the added issue of production and operations departments that may not turn over equipment for maintenance. As a result, many planning and scheduling philosophies take the easy way out and over-schedule work.This leads to frustration on the part of the workforce from never being able to catch up to their daily workload.The result tends to be falling back on performing tasks in the exact amount of time outlined by the task and a growing lethargy,or even unnecessary overtime to meet PM task completion.

In this chapter, we will discuss how to bring these different issues in line in order to develop a consistent strategy to improve your wrench time. The improved efficiency and effectiveness of your maintenance department will provide additional resources from your existing assets, or will help identify the lack of assets that is impacting your company.

6.1 The Workflow Concept

The Workflow Concept (WFC) is derived in the same way that workflow is determined for production, including the methods of Design for Manufacturing and Assembly (DFMA), in which our concept is Design for Maintainability (DFM). Does this refer to changing the design of equipment when it is purchased? Somewhat. However, it also refers to designing the maintenance process around the actual maintenance requirements. In effect, a part of DFM includes such processes as Reliability-Centered Maintenance (RCM) which is a tool used to determine the optimum maintenance for a system.

The concept of RCM provides the information of what the optimal maintenance requirements are, with evidence for that maintenance. The concept of DFM provides the methods for assisting the RCM process in determining budget requirements while also providing information on individual manpower requirements based upon the resources available. It is much like a sports team in that if you coach to a strategy, then your season will be poor; if you coach and develop your strategy to the capabilities of your players, you will do very well. In this case, we are going to look at the capabilities of our personnel and resources and match them to the maintenance development process strategy.

The concepts of WFC and DFM are not unique. They were born of the efforts of production and operations sciences and industrial engineering. The primary difference is we are going to match these traditional manufacturing principles to the application of maintenance scheduling and planning. This is not a significant leap nor is it particularly complex.

Components of the WFC:

1. Determining the maintenance task requirements through processes such as RCM;
2. Performing time and training studies in order to determine the time necessary to perform tasks and to determine optimal methods for performing the tasks;
3. Development of best practices to match the optimal task methods. These should be created in terms of processes and may include times for actual steps;
4. Determine qualifications of individual maintenance personnel for these practices;
5. Benchmark existing or similar best practices and determine the gap between these benchmarks and existing personnel capabilities;

6. Develop goals for the individual personnel based upon the gap; and,
7. Schedule according to the capabilities of personnel.

For the purpose of this chapter, we are going to assume that the RCM process has been completed and we are determining the DFM.

6.2 Time Studies

As explained in Chapter 2, the idea of the time study goes back to the early days of Scientific Management. The idea is to break up a task into manageable chunks and determine the times for each step. The result of a time study can provide the following information:

1. Which tasks, or combination of tasks, can complete the steps the fastest while maintaining quality of work and safety;
2. What resources are required for each portion of the task, including personnel requirements; and,
3. The total man-hours and linear man-hours required to perform the tasks by individual or by projecting based upon experience and training.

Time studies are often seen in a negative light by personnel, leaving it up to the individual manager, or team, to determine the best way to approach this most important step in the maintenance management process. The necessary tools, from a technical standpoint, however, are a timer and a notepad. As we are assuming that such a study has not previously been performed, the notepad should be used to take notes on the individual steps and the times to perform each one. Observations by the analyst should also be noted including the quality and safety aspects of the work being performed.

The analyst must have experience in the types of tasks that are being performed with the optimal person having actually performed the tasks in the past. All records developed must be kept for future analysis to assist in review of the maintenance process through such programs as the Maintenance Effectiveness Review (MER).

A proper time study includes the development of a sampling strategy which includes the number and experience/training of the personnel and the number of task cycles to be studied. This can then be used to develop a minimum, maximum and average task time which is necessary to understand task flow and for scheduling purposes.

The number of task observations, per task, across the experience/training of personnel should be broken into increments and the percentage of each group to the population of personnel should be determined. The number of task observations can be determined as shown in Equations 1 and 2, where:

- ✔ E = Absolute Error
- ✔ p = Percentage occurrence of activity or delay being measured
- ✔ N = The number of random observations (sample size)
- ✔ Z = The number of standard deviations for the desired confidence of the study:
  - ○ Z = 1.65 for 90%
  - ○ Z = 1.96 for 95%
  - ○ Z = 2.23 for 99%

Equation 1   Absolute Error

$$E = \sqrt{\frac{p(1-p)}{N}}$$

Equation 2   Required Sample

$$N = \frac{\left(\dfrac{Z^2 pp(1-p)}{E^2}\right)}{2}$$

For instance, if you have 120 maintenance personnel and you are examining a motor greasing program in which an average of 25 motors are greased in an 8 hour period and you know that the personnel performing the greasing are utilizing approximately 5 hours per day. When reviewed, you have 20 personnel who are fully trained with experience in greasing, 30 who are trained but with only a little experience, 35 who are familiar with motor greasing and 35 who are not. That would be 17% experienced, 25% with some experience; and 29% of each of the others, and then the number of samples would be spread across the appropriate personnel. The Absolute Error would be 9.8% (0.098), when considering all 25 machines and the required sample for 95% confidence would be 49 tasks. If reviewing all 120 personnel, the 49 tasks being studied would be extended as follow:

- ✔ Experienced: 49 * 17% = 8
- ✔ Some Experience: 49 * 25% = 12
- ✔ Familiar: 49 * 29% = 15
- ✔ Unfamiliar: 49 * 29% = 14

The analyst will have to determine which mix of personnel are selected for each of the time studies. This particular approach will also provide us with an estimation of the training gap time from each of the levels to the next, along with training and experience records for each level.

For the time study, itself, a linear breakdown, number of personnel and times for each step of the task should be described and diagramed by the analyst for each of the tasks being reviewed. The actual times are multiplied by a performance rating that may be above or below '1' depending upon the analyst's observation that the observed personnel are working faster or slower than normal.

Using the above example, the tasks for the first experienced maintenance person are determined as follow:

1. The equipment to be greased is tagged out;
2. Grease plugs are removed and a brush inserted to loosen and remove any hardened grease, the grease nipples are cleaned;
3. A measured amount of grease is inserted into the grease nipple;
4. The tag out tag is removed and the motor is operated;

5. The motor is turned off and the grease plugs are re-inserted, then the motor is released for duty.

The times and personnel involved are diagramed as shown in Figure 10.

The total linear time is 3 hours and 10 minutes which deviates significantly from the projected 1 hour and 45 minutes. When the notes from the analyst are reviewed, it is determined that the maintenance person was called away for other tasks and meetings during and between tasks. In the task blocks in Figure 10, the top row

Figure 10: Flow Diagram (PERT Chart)

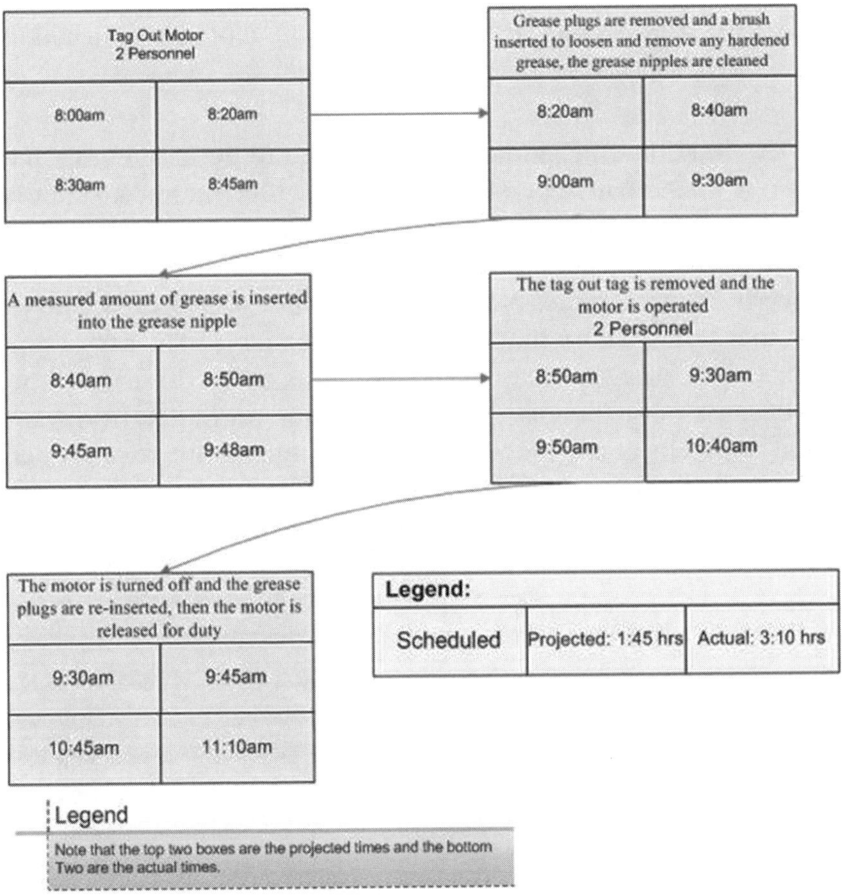

Tag Out Motor 2 Personnel		Grease plugs are removed and a brush inserted to loosen and remove any hardened grease, the grease nipples are cleaned	
8:00am	8:20am	8:20am	8:40am
8:30am	8:45am	9:00am	9:30am

A measured amount of grease is inserted into the grease nipple		The tag out tag is removed and the motor is operated 2 Personnel	
8:40am	8:50am	8:50am	9:30am
9:45am	9:48am	9:50am	10:40am

The motor is turned off and the grease plugs are re-inserted, then the motor is released for duty	
9:30am	9:45am
10:45am	11:10am

Legend:		
Scheduled	Projected: 1:45 hrs	Actual: 3:10 hrs

Legend

Note that the top two boxes are the projected times and the bottom Two are the actual times.

is the projected time for each task and the second row is the actual time in linear hours. The actual man-hours for this task can be determined as 2 hours and 3 minutes for one person and 1 hour and 5 minutes for the second person. In maintenance reviews, this particular experienced maintenance man was determined to be slow.

A second experienced maintenance person is studied. In this case, the maintenance man does not tag out the electric motors or run them after greasing. Instead, his tasks read as follow:

1. The motor is left energized;
2. Grease plugs are removed;
3. Grease is pumped into the bearings until fresh grease shows from the grease plugs;
4. The grease plugs are replaced and the motor is returned to service.

The total time per motor is determined to be 25 minutes and only one maintenance person required. The times across all experienced personnel average out to 1 hour and 46 minutes, close to the original time projected. However, the greasing practices vary between the two extremes noted above. This is also observed with all the other levels, whose times run as shown in Table 6 (Note that normally the average should be weighted but is not in this example).

Because of the dramatic variation in hours, deviation from 9.8% error and steps at each level, a review of industry practices is performed and it is determined that the first example, above (Figure 10) follows the industry best practice. It was also noted that the fastest

Table 6: Direct Calculated Man-Hour Totals

Type of Personnel	Max Total Man-Hours	Min Total Man-Hours	Average
Experienced	3:08 hours	0:25 hours	**1:46 hrs**
Some Experience	3:15 hours	0:40 hours	**1:57 hrs**
Familiar	3:45 hours	1:00 hours	**2:22 hrs**
Unfamiliar	**4:00 hours**	**1:30 hours**	**2:45 hrs**

time (25 minutes) also resulted in the greatest number of bearing failures following greasing PM's. However, the total man-hours benchmarked is the original 1:45 minutes. The analyst reviews the notes and observations and makes the following calculations:

- ✔ Step 1: 0:15 hours * 1 = 0:15 hours
- ✔ Step 2: 0:30 hours * 0.85 = 0:25 hours
- ✔ Step 3: 0:03 hours * 2 = 0:06 hours
- ✔ Step 4: 0:50 hours * 0.85 = 0:42 hours
- ✔ Step 5: 0:25 hours * 0.85 = 0:21 hours

It is also reviewed and determined that the lockout/tagout procedure only requires one maintenance personnel. The same review is given to the rest of the experience levels and the results are shown in Table 7.

As noted, the actual average hours were equal, or close, to the original average hours. This allows the planner/scheduler to view each level of experience with set Upper and Lower Control Limits (UCL/LCL).

6.3 Training/On-The-Job Training and the Gap

With the information shown in the example, along with information on training and experience of the associated personnel, the gap can be evaluated as well as the time to bring less experienced personnel up to speed. For the purposes of the example that we have

Table 7: Modified Man-Hour Totals With Best Practice (3% Error)

Type of Personnel	Max Total Man-Hours	Min Total Man-Hours	Average
Experienced	2:05 hrs	1:35 hrs	1:49 hrs
Some Experience	2:15 hrs	1:40 hrs	1:57 hrs
Familiar	2:45 hrs	2:00 hrs	2:22 hrs
Unfamiliar	3:10 hrs	2:20 hrs	2:45 hrs

been using in this chapter, we will assume that the average training and experience is as follows:

- ✔ Experienced: 2,000 hours lubrication experience and training. Some gap required for some of the personnel once the new greasing best practices have been put in place.
- ✔ Some Experience: 1,000 hours lubrication experience and training.
- ✔ Familiar: 500 hours lubrication experience and training.
- ✔ Unfamiliar: No experience.

Through the development of this curve, the learning gap can be estimated. This is extremely important as it provides evidence of the required training and OJT experience in order to improve times. When planning personnel, it also provides the information necessary to determine the gap between experienced personnel who may be retiring and new personnel hired. This learning curve and the time study should be re-performed at a scheduled point after the best practice has been in place, such as 6 months to a year, in

Figure 11: Experience and Average Hours

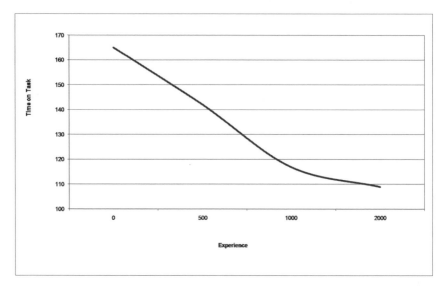

order to measure the impact of the best practice procedure and to correct any errors in the time study.

6.4 Identifying Other Losses

There are a number of losses and concepts for improving the efficiency of tasks, such as the one used as an example in this paper. As part of the exercise of WFC and DFM, the lost time is reviewed and maintenance process design methods are investigated. For this we will introduce a second example before returning to our first one.

In this example, we will consider a motor repair shop department which is a job-shop scheduling environment. The initial study was performed in order to determine why the time per repair was increasing, wrench time was decreasing, on-time deliveries were non-existent and the warranty rate was also increasing. A new supervisor was introduced into the department who had WFC/DFM experience. During 30 days of observation, it was noticed that customer service personnel would bypass the supervisor and approach repair technicians directly throughout all departments, usually their favorite technician regardless of capability and training. The usual instructions were to stop work on one job and start another 'emergency' job at which point work would stop on the task that the technician was working on in order to start another job. In some cases, a few technicians would work on more than one job simultaneously because upper management would approach them directly on their increased times to complete work. The observation was that on 75% of jobs that were interrupted, additional work was missed on disassembly task reports, resulting in improper quotations, and steps were missed in the reassembly of motors resulting in warranty repairs. On jobs that were not interrupted, these issues occurred in less than 1% of the work. The average billable time per technician, in an 8-hour shift, was 4.5 hours, resulting in huge profitability losses and increased operating costs. During this time, the supervisor also evaluated the capabilities of the technicians and performed time studies based upon the time cards turned in for each job. There were 12 customer service reps and 45 shop personnel with 12 being in the supervisor's department.

The new supervisor implemented several best practices that had been observed in other repair shops. All repair requests had to be passed through the supervisor who would then schedule the appropriate personnel to perform the work. Emergency jobs would be scheduled as the next-in-line and/or spread between routine jobs, with past-due jobs receiving priority. No tasks would be interrupted for any reason and a second person had to sign off, as well as the technician, any quality control checks.

In this case, the primary gap had more to do with a culture change. It was also noted that the size of the jobs in the small/medium motor department caused the problems to be more noticeable because of the times and volume of work involved. The supervisor estimated three months to have all the kinks out of the new program during which time he had to deal with customer service personnel complaining to upper management in an attempt to return the environment to where it was. The primary complaint being that they did not feel they were able to meet customer expectations due to scheduling issues.

At the end of the three month gap, the study was performed a second time over a one week period and warranty, time and wrench-time being re-measured. Another study was performed quarterly for the remainder of one year from the implementation of the plan. The first thing that was noticed is that the warranty rate dropped to zero almost immediately on jobs performed following the program implementation. The second thing noticed was that the average wrench time increased to 7.5 hours and average task times dropped by over $1/3^{rd}$ during the first quarter and leveled off at 50% by the end of the year. In effect, throughput increased almost 400% within the first year, and warranty rates were virtually non-existent versus part of the workflow. The concepts gradually flowed throughout the rest of the repair shop departments during the first year and profitability increased dramatically while jobs were being completed on time, and frequently early. As a result, the next step in the process was to make improvements to the scheduling and communication systems between the shop and customer service and sales to improve quoting and delivery times.

Returning to our original example, there are a number of areas for improvement to the workflow to increase wrench time and increase throughput on this particular PM. When reviewing the linear time to correctly perform the best practice, it was determined that burdens were placed upon the individual technicians. While a daily meeting of about 1/2 hour was performed to communicate work, gathering equipment, travel and interruptions took up the remainder of the estimated 2.5 hours. In fact, it could be considered that the estimated 5 hours wrench time was overestimated.

The analyst reviews the workflow and notes taken during the 49 observations performed. In this, it is determined that maintenance personnel are contacted directly by customers and managers pull the technicians off of jobs, and they are sometimes made to wait, or are turned away, for production reasons. At the present time, individual machines are greased from start to finish before moving on to the next one, in a job-shop type process. The analyst reviews the list of work and determines the following DFM strategy:

1. Convert from a job-shop process and perform greasing from a batch process. This means that instead of tagging out and greasing one motor at a time, a group of motors is tagged out logistically close to each other, and the greasing procedure applied simultaneously on each batch. The number of motors for each batch is determined by location and availability to perform the tasks. Each group is broken out into individual work orders and the time to perform each group is monitored and scheduled for time study.

2. All communications with the maintenance personnel must be directed through the planner/scheduler. The planner/scheduler has access to the capabilities of each maintenance technician and their experience related to the training gap chart.

It is determined that there are ten machines in an average group. Time studies show that the average time to grease a batch of ten motors is four linear/man-hours for the experienced technicians. This reduces the number of technicians greasing motors from 3 motors per experienced technician per day, or an average of 6 experienced persons greasing motor per day, to an average of 2 experienced technicians per day (with variations due to batch sizes). Task completion improves dramatically and additional personnel are available for other tasks.With the reduction of interruptions, the average wrench time improves to 6.5 hours, or 30%, resulting in a wrench time of 81.3% up from 62.5% related to this task.The remaining time is dedicated to the daily meetings, travel and materials.

6.5 The Reactive Maintenance Process

The other type of maintenance that occurs, regardless of the type of program that is in place, is reactive maintenance as the result of random failure.All systems have the chance of failing unexpectedly, so methods must be in place to handle these situations in order to have the least impact on the planning and scheduling process.

Where programs are advancing towards higher levels of maintenance, random equipment failure can be an opportunity for maintenance. However, the reaction is often to over-react and over provide resources to the problem at hand.The challenge is that too few resources, or too many resources will both have the same negative impact on solving the reactive issue.The opportunity can be outlined in a reactive maintenance plan for specific equipment in which there is a method of fault detection, fault rectification, root-cause-analysis at whatever level is appropriate, and planned maintenance to be performed when the machine or system is idle.

Once a system or component ceases to perform the function required by the owner, the equipment is considered to have failed.At this point, the random fault has occurred with an urgency based upon the criticality of the equipment. The correct process to address the failure is as follows:

1. Fault Identification:At this point, discovery of the fault occurs, the failure is controlled and troubleshooting is performed;
2. Fault Rectification:This is the repair or replacement of the failure;
3. Root-Cause-Analysis: Using the evidence and findings of the fault and fault rectification, an RCA should be performed.The depth of the RCA should directly relate to the criticality. For instance, for a minor failure that is not repetitive or does not meet a pre-set value, a simple 5-Why process may be fol-

lowed. For a critical failure, or one that exceeds a pre-set value, a more rigorous process should be followed.

4. Additional planned maintenance that can be performed on the faulted equipment should be considered a possibility. This may include additional testing to detect latent problems.

In order to ensure that these steps are performed as effectively as possible, a written process must be developed.

6.6 Fault Identification

Troubleshooting equipment or system failure can be time consuming and dependent upon the skills and knowledge the maintenance first responders. Knowing the available skills the maintenance planner can select the appropriate first-responders. The challenge is then left to troubleshooting and the correct selection of inspection and technology techniques.

The tools that can be used to determine the appropriate troubleshooting and inspection techniques include the results from Reliability-Centered Maintenance (the Failure Modes and Effects Analysis), a Failure Modes, Effects and Criticality Analysis (FMECA), the manufacturers' manuals, historical data, knowledge capture and/or other processes such as Root-Cause-Analysis studies. The results of each of these opportunities should be put in the form of a logic analysis or troubleshooting chart.

The development of such a chart involves, first, a combination of the above information as well as the instrumentation available and the abilities of the maintenance personnel. Such a chart provides direct troubleshooting abilities as well as provides confirmation tests, inspections and pass/fail values. The long-term benefit of such charts, in particular for critical machines, is greater control over the time, effort and selection of skills through the understanding of the length of time such tasks should take. This information can come from the time studies performed for preventive maintenance.

It should be noted that some failures will require efforts well beyond the ability of these charts, which would instead provide a guideline. However, they will reduce the time to troubleshoot and bring a system back online quicker, controlling the impact of random failures as well as providing information on the number, type and capability of personnel required.

6.7 Fault Rectification

The fault rectification process requires that repair specifications are developed for outsourced repair, internal best practices/procedures for common fault repair or replacement. The development of an overall spares identification program combined with agreements with vendors will also provide a level of stability and control over the random failure.

Fault rectification information can be an extension to the troubleshooting charts mentioned in the previous section. The development of the process/procedures will assist in the development of training, the selection of vendors and an early indication when outsourcing is required.

6.8 Additional Planned Maintenance

As part of the Reactive Maintenance Plan, any additional planned maintenance should be added. For instance, if a fan system motor fails, inspection of belts, sheaves, fan bearings, cleanliness, and other inspections can be performed. These should be planned around the availability of the personnel assigned to the random fault as, much of the time, personnel are on location, they are idle. Random faults should be considered an opportunity to inspect and improve availability of the system once it comes back online.

6.9 Time Planning of Reactive Maintenance

Random faults should be considered a 'job shop' style process and qualifies for the application of a Critical Path Method (CPM) for determining how much time is required to perform the maintenance, especially because there can be a minimum and maximum time for each sub-task. The times for the CPM should be obtained from the time studies performed for preventive maintenance plus any historical times. The three times selected for each branch of the CPM are the fastest, average and slowest.

In this example, we will discuss a 500 horsepower electric motor and pump application. The motor fails to start and trips immediately. The trouble chart is reviewed and a technician with an MCA (Motor Circuit Analysis) device is sent out as well as a second technician to check the pump seal packing and the alignment if the motor winding is good. The motor is checked from the starter, following appropriate safety rules, a problem is found, so the motor connection box is open, the connection split and both the cable and motor are tested. In the meantime, the second technician is checking the packing. The cable is found bad and new cable is obtained. Once the material is provided, both technicians are used to install the new cable and the machine is energized. The 5-Why analysis is performed and it is determined that a previous FMEA did not identify cable testing as a requirement on this machine. It is determined, however, that the test is not cost effective on its own, and it is determined that MCA will be performed on a quarterly basis.

In a PERT chart, three numbers are shown associated with each task. These are: The minimum time, the average time and the maximum time. The CPM is then presented as shown in Figure 12. The advantage of this type of chart is that it can be hand-sketched if one does not already exist.

While this example is very simple, it does demonstrate the process. In fact, it now gives us three numbers associated with the reactive fault: Minimum—95 minutes; Average—180 Minutes; and, Maximum - 290 Minutes. We also know that the number of personnel required for this project is two.

Figure 12: Sample PERT Chart (CPM)

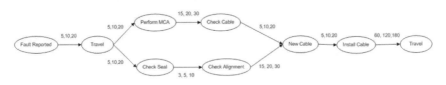

6.10 Blending the Planned Maintenance Program and the Reactive Maintenance Plan

When considering the overall planning and scheduling process, an idea of the amount of reactive maintenance time, or random failure time, must be determined as well as when they are most likely to occur by estimating equipment failure. There are a great many ways in which this may be determined, and most of those require a great deal of resources in order to come up with accurate measures. However, simple processes used in production/operations and finance referred to as forecasting can be used to provide a reasonably accurate idea of what and when issues may occur within a calculated error range.

The forecasting process is used in the WFC (Work-Flow Concept) and DFM (Design for Maintenance) methods in order to provide guidance to the planner/scheduler in identifying the most likely times that systems may fail and may be utilized on both critical and non-critical equipment in order to provide an additional layer to spares inventory and budgeting. In this section, we are going to discuss forecasting, how it may be used to model a variety of concepts within the maintenance organization, then how it is used to determine resources and as a maintenance tool.

In a static maintenance environment, or one in which no new maintenance initiatives are being implemented, the concept of forecasting for random failures and reactive maintenance is straight forward and the time will usually be increasing. There are two methods that can be used for forecasting the maintenance process including the weighted moving average and linear regression. These are both measurement-based methods requiring that the user determine if they are going to base the forecast on a time-scale or production-scale. For instance, if the random failures seem to be more or less predictable regardless of production levels, then the user may wish to use a time-based system (i.e.: Failure Rate in Hours). If the random failures seem to follow increases and decreases in production levels, then the user may wish to use a production-based system (i.e.: Failure Rate in Units of Production).

There are several basic steps to the process that must be understood before actually applying the selected forecasting method:

1. What time-frame is the forecast being applied across? How far out is it going to be applied? This is important as the further you move out, in time or production, the greater the error will be.
2. Are there specific patterns to the random failure history? Are the patterns based upon the time of year? Time of day? Units of production? This information is used to determine the forecasting method in use.
3. There is an assumption that in a static system the total cost and resources to maintain the system will be increasing over time. Is this the case?

The first process that we will use will be the weighted moving average. For this process, a multiplier is used for history and applied via a formula, as follows:

Equation 3   Weighted Moving Average

$$F = 0.4(P4) + 0.3(P3) + 0.2(P2) + 0.1(P1)$$

Where F = the Forecast and P = the Period in Question

For example, if the forecast is being performed for the quarter, the history of the past four quarters is required. As in Table 8, the latest period is the highest number:

Table 8: Example of Hours
of Random Failure Per Quarter

Quarter (Period)	Random Failure Hours
1	25
2	27
3	30
4	29

The weighted average for the next quarter would be:

Equation 4   Weighted Moving Average Applied (Example 1)

$$F = 0.4(29) + 0.3(30) + 0.2(27) + 0.1(25) = 28 \text{ } hours$$

Based upon the moving weighted average, 28.5 hours should be forecast for the next quarter in reactive maintenance.

Now, let's see how a more dynamic example will apply:

Table 9, Example 2: Hours of Random Failure
Per 1,000 Units Manufactured

1,000 of Units	Random Failure Hours
1	20
2	44
3	38
4	12

Equation 5   Weighted Moving Average Applied (Example 2)

$$F = 0.4(12) + 0.3(38) + 0.2(44) + 0.1(20) = 27 \text{ } hours$$

As you can see, in the first example, the value given provides some level of accuracy that can have a specified error that would be acceptable. However, in the second example, you will notice that the value may not represent what may happen through random failures. The error has the potential of being too high. In this case, let us explore another level to the weighted average called 'exponential smoothing.'

Table 10: Example of Exponential
Smoothing from Example 2

1,000 of Units	Random Failure Hours
1	20
2	44
3	38
4	12
5	42

In our original forecast for example 2, we came up with a value of 27 hours of reactive maintenance. Now, using exponential smoothing from Equation 6, we can use the error to predict the next random failure period.

Equation 6   Exponential Smoothing

$$F = F_{T-1} + \alpha (A_{T-1} - F_{T-1})$$

Where F is the forecast for the next period, F_{T1}
is the forecast for the last period

α is the smoothing constant and A_{T1} is the actual failure
for period T-1

The smoothing constant represents a percentage of the forecast error. For the third example, we will determine the exponentially smoothed forecast for the sixth batch of 1,000 units: The error was (27/42 = 0.643), so the next forecast will be: F = (27 + 0.643(42-27) = 36.6 hours. This method is then applied for the next period, and so on.

Another method of forecasting involves the use of simple linear regression in which a line is fixed to a set of points. The basic format for the simple linear regression technique is shown in Equation 7.

Equation 7   Simple Linear Regression Formula

$$y_c = a + bx$$

$$b = \frac{n\left(\sum xy\right) - \left(\sum x\right) - \left(\sum y\right)}{n\left(\sum x^2\right) - \left(\sum x\right)^2}$$

$$a = \frac{\sum y - b\sum x}{n}$$

Where y_c is the estimated variable, x is the estimator,
b is the slope of the line and a is the value of y_c
when $x = 0$ on a graph, n is number of paired observations.

Table 11: Forecast of Reactive
Maintenance Per Week

Week	Random Failure Hours
1	5
2	6
3	5
4	7
5	8
6	6
7	8
8	9
9	7
10	9

The assumption for the linear regression is that points tend to develop around a straight line. So, with values such as those in Table 11, we can develop an analysis of forecast beyond the next period.

With this information, we can determine all of the X and Y needed for the formulae, as shown in Table 12.

These values can then be plugged in to the formulae in equation 7.

Equation 8   Solution for b (Example 3)

$$b = \frac{10(417) - (55)(70)}{10(385) - 55^2} = 0.388$$

Equation 9   Solution for a (Example 3)

$$a = \frac{70 - 0.388(55)}{10} = 4.87$$

Equation 10   Solution for Linear Regression (Example 3)

$$y_c = 4.87 + 0.388x$$

Table 12: Linear Regression Calculations

x	y	xy	x^2	y^2
1	5	5	1	25
2	6	12	4	36
3	5	15	9	25
4	7	28	16	49
5	8	40	25	64
6	6	36	36	36
7	8	56	49	64
8	9	72	64	81
9	7	63	81	49
10	9	90	100	81
SUM = 55	SUM = 70	SUM = 417	SUM = 385	SUM = 510

With this information, we can determine what is going to happen in the following weeks. For instance, if we were to estimate reactive maintenance hours for week 12, the answer would be $y_c =$ 4.87 + (0.388)(12) = 9.5 hours. As you progress, you need to determine the actual hours and re-establish the linear regression to represent a more accurate view of conditions.

6.11 Forecasting Error

The use of forecasting error methods is to be able to evaluate the methods used and to compare them to other methods to see which one is the best process. The two common methods are MAD (Mean Absolute Deviation) and MSE (Mean Squared Error) where MAD is the average absolute error and MSE is the average of squared errors. For the purposes of this demonstration, we are going to work with the MAD method (Equation 11).

Equation 11   MAD Forecasting Error Method

$$MAD = \frac{\sum |actual - forecast|}{n}$$

Table 13: Table of Errors Using Weighted Average (Example 4)

Week	Random Failure Hours (Actual)	Forecast (Weighted Average)	Error	[Error]
1	5			
2	6			
3	5			
4	7			
5	8	6	2	2
6	6	6.9	−0.9	0.9
7	8	6.7	1.3	1.3
8	9	7.3	1.7	1.7
9	7	8	−1	1
10	9	7.7	1.3	1.3
		SUM = 42.6	SUM = 4.4	SUM = 8.2

Using the MAD method for determining error, the error averages (4.4/6 = 0.73 hours) which is a pretty good forecast.

6.12 The Average Cost Impact of Maintenance Programs Multiplier

In the introduction of this book, we discussed the impact of different levels of maintenance in a cost($)/horsepower/year for a facility. These values, as shown in Figure 13, represent the potential impact of moving from one type of maintenance to the next. This information can be used in lieu of actual values, if you do not have a history of the impact of different programs.

The values are used as multipliers. For instance, if I am developing a predictive maintenance program from a reactive maintenance program, the impact would be (8/18)*100% or 44.4% times cost or hours.

6.13 Probability of Equipment Survival

In addition to the forecast of hours, there is a need to estimate the equipment that will be affected. For this part, history and some gut

Figure 13: Cost Impact of Maintenance Programs

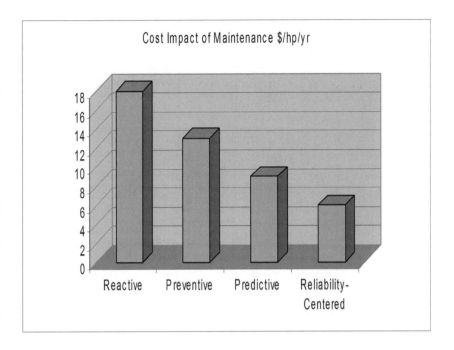

Cost Impact of Maintenance $/hp/yr

assumptions may have to be made. The more history and detail that is available, the more accurate your equipment forecasts will be. A few of the assumptions we will make in this section include:

- ✔ The equipment failure rate will, more or less, follow a normalized bell curve. This allows easy use of MTBF and MTTR values;
- ✔ The process will be a combination of series and parallel systems.

Using historical data, records, manufacturing data, etc., we need to determine the following:

1. Mean Time Between Failure (MTBF) or Mean Time To Repair (MTTR) by taking the total time of operation in hours, days, weeks or whatever your preference is, and divide by the number of failures;

2. Determine the Failure Rate, which is 1/MTBF or 1/MTTR;
3. Keep these values as high up the system as makes sense for modeling different maintenance practices; and,
4. Start by obtaining the extremes—Failure Rates for the systems if no maintenance is performed and the failure rates if all recommended maintenance is performed. Then any fine-tuning can be determined.

In the next step, make a block diagram of the system with identified failure rates for each part that is identified. We can now apply all of the data through a set of simple formulae known as the Reliability Function, The Series Reliability Function and the Parallel Reliability Functions.

Equation 12   The Reliability Function

$$R = e^{-t\lambda}$$

Where e is the natural log, t is the time of interest (must be the same as what was used to determine the failure rate), and λ is the failure rate.

The Reliability Function shown in Equation 12 is the chance of survival for the system at a particular time.

Equation 13   The Series Reliability Function

$$R_s = (R_a)(R_b) \ldots (R_n)$$

Equation 14   Two-System Parallel Reliability

$$R_p = (R_a + R_b) - (R_a)(R_b)$$

Equation 15   The Parallel Reliability for Three or More Identical Systems

$$R_p = 1 - (1 - R)^n$$

Where n is the number of parallel systems.

Table 14: Breakdown of Components and Failure Rates

Component	Failure Rate (per hour)	Days for Repair
Bus	2.0×10^{-5}	5
Controls	3.3×10^{-5}	0.5
Float Switch System	6.7×10^{-5}	2
Pump	2.1×10^{-5}	5
Piping and Valves	2.5×10^{-5}	5
Tank	1.0×10^{-5}	20

When calculating through, determine the survivability of the parallel system first, then the series system. For instance, in a simple pump system, as follows:

There is a sump system where, if the level exceeds 10 feet, or the tank wall ruptures, it has failed. Because of the critical nature of the system, there are redundant submersible pumps. Both pumps are 'hard-piped' to a common outlet with backflow valves on each one. Both submersibles are fed by separate starters and float switches. The starters are fed from a common bus. It has been determined that maintenance practices and inspections will identify 90% of faults allowing for scheduled shutdowns.

Breakdown of the system, the failure rate in hours and the availability of parts and time to repair are listed in Table 14.

The failure rates can also be presented in terms of what is being used for forecasting time, in order to make modeling scenarios similar. In this case, however, if we were to evaluate the system for 6,000 hours (3 shifts, 5 days per week), we would end up with a system as represented in Figure 14.

At the 6,000 hour point of operation, this system has a 58.2% chance of survival.

6.14 Modeling Systems for Accurate Planning and Scheduling

With the above information we can begin to model scenarios for improving our planning and scheduling. Some of the additional

Figure 14: Pumping System Example

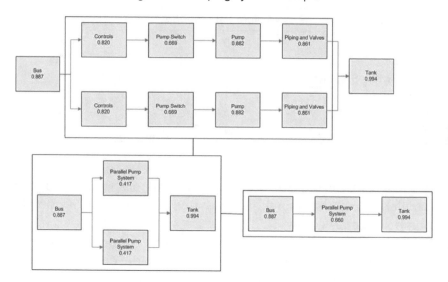

information that we will need to determine include the lag times for the implementation of maintenance strategies. However, with the information provided in this chapter, we can begin to look at our resource and manpower needs. The extent of such modeling can be as intense or as simple as is required.

For example, we will take a 4,000 hour per year production line. The process manufactures and packages cookies and consists of the following components:

1. Incoming electrical power;
2. Controls;
3. Measuring and Mixing machines;
4. A steam system;
5. An oven and conveyor system for cooking;
6. A cooling system;
7. A quality control system, pre-packaging;
8. Packaging;
9. A quality control system, post-packaging.

Additionally, there are the following systems:

1. Storage and truck unloading;
2. Compressed air product transfer systems;
3. Building lighting systems;
4. HVAC systems;
5. Office systems and other systems will not be addressed at this time;
6. Facilities and cleaning systems;
7. Fire protection systems;
8. Other.

There are four industrial electricians (two per shift), four mechanical tradesmen and two general trades. Three of the four electricians are considered experienced and the fourth is new, with the same ratio for the four mechanical trades. The two general trades are considered laborers with a medium level of skill. A janitorial staff maintains the cleanliness of the building. While critical systems are automatically assigned planned and reactive maintenance programs, we cannot forget the run-to-failure systems.

The complete system is on a planned maintenance program only.

The tradesmen have an estimated wrench-time of 6 hours per shift, or 30 hours per week, which is exceptional in that travel time and wait times are considered nil, for this model. The questions are:

1. What is the projected time of the 30 hours required for random failures for each tradesperson in week 11? The remaining time is the time that can be scheduled for general predictive maintenance.
2. What systems are projected to have the highest chance of random failure during that week? This allows the planner to rate the correct parts and vendor availability.

Through linear regression we are able to determine that mechanical has 9.14 hours and electrical has 16.9 hours. If spread

Table 15: Reliability of Plant Systems

Component	Failure Rate (per hour)	Operating Hours (End of Week 11)	Critical?	Days for Repair
Transformer and Switchgear	1.3×10^{-5}	5,000	Y	1
MCC for each line	6.7×10^{-5}	2,500	Y	0.5
Controls (Measure and Mix)	6.7×10^{-5}	1,500	Y	1
Measure and Mix Equipment	4.0×10^{-5}	3,000	Y	2
Controls (Steam System)	1.3×10^{-4}	500	Y	1
Steam System (Boiler)	2.0×10^{-5}	3,300	Y	5
Oven and Cooking System	1.7×10^{-4}	0	Y	1
Chiller System	5.0×10^{-5}	1,000	Y	2
Refrigeration/ Cooling	1.7×10^{-4}	6,000	Y	3
Quality Control Equipment	2.5×10^{-4}	100	Y	0.5
Packaging System	6.7×10^{-4}	800	Y	1
Storage and Truck Unloading	5.0×10^{-4}	1,000	Y	1
Compressed Air System	5.0×10^{-4}	100	Y	1.5
Building Lighting	1.0×10^{-2}	–	N	0
HVAC	5.0×10^{-4}	600	N	1

across all four mechanicals, then $(120 - 9.14)/4 = 27.7$ PM hours in week 11 each and 25.8 PM hours in week 11 for the electricians.

The highest chance for failures are considered based upon the existing hours on Table 8, which are the end of the week on week 10 (Table 16). Week 11 includes the additional 80 hours. The order of potential failure is as follows:

By taking each system down closer to the component level, the actual types of faults can be estimated.

Table 16: Unscheduled Downtime By Trade-Type
(80 hour week / 2 × 40 hour shifts)

Week	Random Failure Hours (Electrical)	Random Failure Hours (Mechanical)
1	8	5
2	7	6
3	9	5
4	10	7
5	12	8
6	11	6
7	15	8
8	12	9
9	13	7
10	18	9

Table 17: Survival Through Week 11 (Lowest to Highest)

Component	Failure Rate (per hour)	Operating Hours	Survival Week 11
Refrigeration/Cooling	1.7×10^{-4}	6,080	0.361
Packaging System	6.7×10^{-4}	880	0.555
Storage and Truck Unloading	5.0×10^{-4}	1,080	0.583
HVAC	5.0×10^{-4}	680	0.712
MCC for each line	6.7×10^{-5}	2,580	0.846
Measure and Mix Equipment	4.0×10^{-5}	3,080	0.887
Controls (Measure and Mix)	6.7×10^{-5}	1,580	0.904
Compressed Air System	5.0×10^{-4}	180	0.914
Controls (Steam System)	1.3×10^{-4}	580	0.927
Steam System (Boiler)	2.0×10^{-5}	3,380	0.934
Transformer and Switchgear	1.3×10^{-5}	5,080	0.936
Chiller System	5.0×10^{-5}	1,080	0.951
Quality Control Equipment	2.5×10^{-4}	180	0.975
Oven and Cooking System	1.7×10^{-4}	80	0.986

Chapter 7

A Few Maintenance Philosophies

There are a number of maintenance philosophies meant for the development and continuous improvement of general maintenance programs. With most of them coming into being starting in the 1960's, their focus has been to focus maintenance strategies on critical equipment. These philosophies include, but are not limited to, Reliability-Centered Maintenance (RCM), Total Quality Management (TQM), Six-Sigma, Lean Maintenance and Total Productive Maintenance (TPM). For the purposes of this book, we will focus on the Classical RCM Process.

7.1 Classical Maintenance

An oft-misunderstood concept is that of the philosophy of maintenance, with many different definitions being presented by any variety of 'experts.' For the purpose of this book, we will define maintenance as actions taken to ensure that components, equipment and systems provide their intended functions when required.[23] To understand this definition, we will briefly study the concepts built into the statement including understanding what is meant by systems and intended functions.

---

[23] NAVSEA MIL-P-24534A, US Navy (MIL-P).

Early maintenance tasks were simple, such as maintaining a cart, plow or simple tools. In all cases, they had a useful life prior to wearing out and either requiring replacement or significant repair. The length of life, or Mean Time Between Failure (MTBF), varied based upon use and individual craftsmanship. With the industrial revolution, systems became more and more complex and more specific skills were required to maintain the systems. Each component of the system has a different wear rate of different types making maintenance scheduling and reliability significantly complex. As a result, failures of these complex systems are fairly random.

So, why then do we do maintenance? We do maintenance because we believe that hardware reliability degrades with age, but we can do something to restore or maintain the original reliability that pays for itself. As such, the basic requirement of maintenance is to preserve function, not necessarily the design intention, of systems. Therefore, being able to define and identify the function of a system is essential prior to selecting any type of maintenance task.

The function of an item or system is defined as any action or operation which that item is intended to perform, or its performance capability.[24] Functions can be broken down into six classifications:

- Active: Requires activity of the component or system. For instance, the active function of an electric motor is to convert electrical energy to mechanical torque.
- Passive: Requires the component or system to be inactive. For instance, the passive function of the electric motor is to contain electrical power using insulation systems.
- Evident: The loss of function is observable to the operator(s). For example: The motor stops running.
- Hidden: Provided by a component or system for which there is no immediate indication of malfunction or failure. Demand for the function(s) usually follows another failure or unexpected event. For example: The contacts are welded shut on a motor starter such that when the motor is de-energized, or

---

[24]MIL-P.

trips, power continues to be provided to the motor in one or more phases.

- Online: Continuously or continually provided during normal operations.
- Offline: Not continuously or continually provided during normal operations. Activated by some other action or event.

7.2 Maintenance Mindset, Failure and Risk

The most common maintenance mindset is that all failures can and must be prevented. The concept is that risk avoidance of all systems is good maintenance. Within this concept, however, a great deal of time and energy is spent on all systems, which usually leads to a reactive maintenance condition. Reactive maintenance is simply defined as maintenance that is driven by functional failures of systems and components, with little or no ability to plan maintenance tasks.

The correct mindset should be that not all failures can or should be prevented. Risk management is actually considered good maintenance. This risk should be directly related to the functional requirements of the system. Not all failures need to be prevented.

Failure, itself, is the presence of unsatisfactory conditions within the system. Hidden failures are not evident to operators when they occur. The typically involve as special feature such as a safety or protective device. Multiple failures must occur to create a significant problem. Consideration is given such that both severity and probability of failure must be evaluated objectively for best long term results. It is known that every failure involves a risk, but not all failures have the same risk and some failures are simply not worth preventing.

Equation 16: Risk

$$Risk = P_f x S_f$$

Values can be put to both P_f (Probability of Failure) and S_f (Severity of Failure), such as shown in Table 18. Selected maintenance

Table 18: Probability and Severity

Score	Probability (Frequency of Event)	Severity (Consequence of Event)		
		Safety	Production	Economic
5	Event will happen in normal operations	Any personnel safety consequence could result in death	Production effectiveness is lost	No Score. Not equivalent to safety
4	Event very likely to occur in time but not certain that occurrence will happen in normal operations	May cause severe injury or severe occupational illness	Production effectiveness is degraded	Repairs are required causing severe economic effects
3	Event may occur in time	May cause minor injury or minor illness	No effect on Production but equipment failure causes system failure	Repairs may be required or deferred causing substantial economic effects
2	Event can occur in normal operations but not likely	Probably would not affect personnel but still a violation of standards	No effect on Production but equipment failure causes system degradation	Repairs may be deferred causing limited effects
1	Event should not occur in normal operations	No hazards will result from event occurring	No hazards will result from event occurring	No hazards will result from event occurring

tasks must pay for themselves with value added determined, as priorities:

1. Safety: Must be a top priority, in all cases.
2. Regulatory: Laws and regulations.
3. Production.
4. Cost Effectiveness.

An example of an effective comparative table can be found in Table 19.

7.3 Types of Maintenance and Maintenance Tasks

The next step to understanding maintenance is understanding the types of maintenance. In the case of classical maintenance, there are three basic types:

- Corrective: Lost or degraded functions restored by correcting unsatisfactory conditions. Corrective action on an electric

Table 19: Risk Table

5	5	10	15	20	25
4	4	8	12	16	20
3	3	6	9	12	15
2	2	4	6	8	10
1	1	2	3	4	5
	1	2	3	4	5

Table 20: Consequence of Event

▓▓▓	<4	Trivial	Acceptable Risk: Change in frequency or to maintenance action is required
▒▒▒	4-6	Low Risk	Change in frequency or modification of the maintenance action is preferred
☐	8-12	Moderate Risk	Change in frequency or modification of the maintenance action is possible
▒▒▒	15-16	Significant Risk	More detailed assessment required before changing frequency or maintenance action
▓▓▓	>16	Extreme Risk	Unacceptable risk. No change in frequency or maintenance action is acceptable

motor might include: Rewind; Bearing replacement; Machining; and/or, Clean, dip and bake.

- Preventive: Minimize conditions that cause unsatisfactory degradation of function. Preventive tasks include predictive maintenance, testing, lubrication, etc.
- Redesign: Eliminate a specific unsatisfactory condition by altering the design of the item. This an include replacing a DC machine with an AC machine, changing the drive end bearing of a motor from ball to roller bearings for a belted application, etc.

For the purpose of this book, we will focus on Preventive Maintenance. Within this category, there are five preventive maintenance task types:

1. Condition Directed: Condition-Based Monitoring, also known as Predictive Maintenance (PdM).
2. Time Directed: Periodic corrections or general maintenance such as replacing components regardless of condition.
3. Failure Finding: Includes such tasks as a visual inspection of contacts in a starter or looking for loose connections.

Table 21: Types of Maintenance

Type of Maintenance	Corrective	Preventive	Redesign
Objective and Characteristic Action	Correct unsat conditions: • Replace components • Adjust or align; • Other	Minimize unsat conditions: • Diagnose condition: Inspect and test • Pre-empt wear out: Restore or replace • Check hidden functions • Lubricate • Service	Eliminate unsat conditions: • **Modify to meet actual requirements** • **Upgrade to meet new specifications**
Scheduling	Unplanned	Planned (Recurring Action)	**Planned (One-Time Action)**
Examples	• **Rewind** • **Clean, dip and bake** • **Bearing replacement**	• **Condition Based Monitoring** • **Oil or grease** • **Visual inspections**	• **Replace ball bearing with roller bearing** • **Install VFD** • **Install single phase protection**

4. Servicing: Includes such tasks as topping off fluids, etc.
5. Lubrication: Bearing greasing, etc.

All of these maintenance tasks must be relevant in order to add value. If a task does not meet a need, or aggravates other unsatisfactory conditions, it must be eliminated.

EMD technologies, such as MCA and ESA, are considered Condition-Based Monitoring tasks. The reason is that these technologies are capable of detecting equipment unsatisfactory conditions early enough, in most cases, to be able to perform corrective action. Even though not all conditions will be detected, as all failures are random, a vast majority of conditions occur gradually.

In the past, with simple systems, it was determined that equipment would have an infant mortality (high rate of failure after being put into service), a fairly steady reliability over its life, then a gradual wear out period (high rate of failure towards the end of life).

Figure 15: Hardware Age Chart

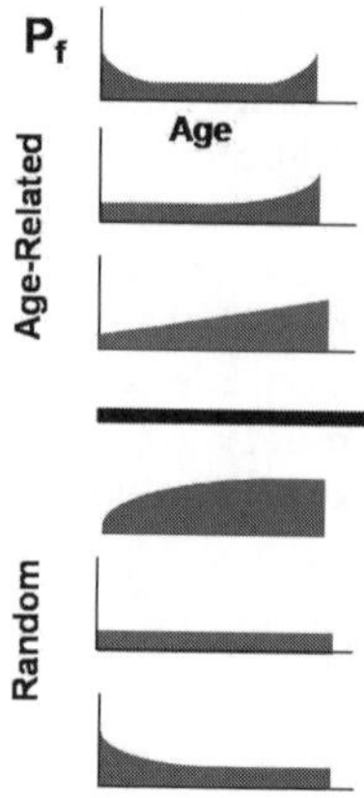

		UAL 1968	Broberg 1973	MSDP Studies 1983	SSMD 1993
A.		4%	3%	3%	6%
B.		2%	1%	17%	0%
C.		5%	4%	3%	0%
D.		7%	11%	6%	0%
E.		14%	15%	42%	60%
F.		68%	66%	29%	33%
		89%	92%	77%	93%

Each complex system will consist of many age-related and random failure curves. As a result, a number of the issues within a system, such as a motor system, can be evaluated by condition and corrected, as necessary. The frequency of testing, using CBM, should be applied as shown in Figure 16. For instance, if a winding short can be detected about six months from absolute failure, the frequency of testing should be at least once per quarter.

7.4 Classical RCM

Reliability Centered Maintenance (RCM) can be defined as a process to ensure that the right maintenance is performed on the right equipment at the right time. The concept was first initiated by the FAA and US-based airlines in the 1960's as a measure to investigate cost effective methods for improving aircraft maintenance costs without sacrificing safety. United Airlines began their initial efforts with the joint task force to assist in selecting reasonable maintenance practices for the new Boeing 747, which was to be released in 1968. The primary issue was that with existing FAA regulations, the 747 would spend more time in maintenance than in service. The

Figure 16: Winding Short CBM Example

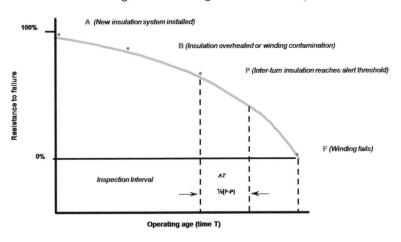

concepts brought about by the airline identified that not only could maintenance practices undergo a major overhaul in frequency, but that a significant number of component and system failures were a direct result of too-frequent maintenance. The US military tasked F. Stanley Nowlan and Howard F. Heap, both of United Airlines, to develop a process which was published as the Reliability-Centered Maintenance report (commonly referred to as the 'Nowlan and Heap') in December of 1978. The US Navy adopted the concept of RCM via the MIL-P-24534A (MIL-P), which mandated RCM for all Navy preventive maintenance system development. The latest edition (at the time of this book) was published in 1983.

Nowlan and Heap defined RCM as: "A logical discipline for developing a scheduled maintenance program that will realize the inherent reliability levels of complex equipment at minimum cost." The Navy MIL-P defines it as: "A method for determining preventive maintenance requirements based on the analysis of the likely functional failures of hardware having a significant impact on safety, operations and support functions."

Since this time, a large variety of 'flavors' of RCM have come available, such as RCM II and other disciplines. These systems have come into being in order to provide a more 'rigorous' approach with roots in the original system, and with their own language and philosophy. While this book will not spend time commenting on these different methods, it is fair to note that most of these processes are very time-intensive. At the time of this book, the only method that has a certification associated with it is the Classical RCM (MIL-P) method, through NAVSEA, as well as the 'Backfit RCM' method.

The Backfit RCM method was actually devised through the military arm of the American Management Systems (AMS) consulting group as a method of performing a 'maintenance effectiveness review' of existing systems and as a method of following up on RCM programs after they have been implemented.

7.5 The Classical RCM Process

The benefit of the Classical RCM process is that it can be used as simply or as complex as is necessary to fit the needs of the analyst. There are seven questions that the RCM process is designed to apply:

1. What are the functions and associated desired standards of performance of the asset in its present operating context (functions)?
2. In what ways can it fail to fulfill its functions (functional failures)?
3. What causes each functional failure (failure modes)?
4. What happens when each failure occurs (failure effects)?
5. In what way does each failure matter (failure consequences)?
6. What should be done to predict or prevent each failure (proactive tasks and task intervals)?
7. What should be done if a suitable proactive task cannot be found (default actions)?

In order to provide a comprehensive, though simple, process requires that boundaries are established and that the interfaces, both coming in and going out, and components of the system are identified. For instance, if you were to place your boundaries around the electric motor only, you would have supply voltage and current limits as an in-interface and the torque and speed as an out interface.

The components might include the housing, bearings, machine fits, rotor, stator, and the rotor and stator windings.

The following definitions are required for RCM:

1. Function: The task that the system or component is required to perform.
2. Functional Failure: When a system or component ceases to provide a required function.
3. Failure Modes: The specific condition causing a functional failure.
4. Failure Cause: The condition that precipitates the failure mode.
5. Failure Effects: Are the consequences of a failure mode. This is evaluated at three levels:
   o Locally where the failure mode occurs,
   o At the system or subsystem level, and,
   o The end effect.

The consequences are used to assist in determining if CBM tasks are effective, combined with understanding the risks involved.

Chapter 8

Business Impact of Maintenance Programs (Summary)

In 2005, the direct costs for R&M was estimated at $1.2 Trillion of which $750 Billion is due to improper asset management. Even though companies have continued to cut R&M manpower, in an effort to reduce costs, the direct investment has continued to rise. The indirect costs, such as lost opportunity, unplanned outages and all other costs associated with poor maintenance practices also continues to rise and represented 20% of the $12.5 Trillion USD GDP in 2005, or $2.5 Trillion. In effect, poor maintenance management practices have been extremely poor business investments.

The asset management strategies of slash and burn maintenance budgets or reactive maintenance have surpassed the point of easy recovery for most companies. The common practice has degenerated, in most maintenance communities, to 'hero maintenance.' In this style of maintenance, when things go wrong the maintenance staff swoops in, makes things work and fly out again. Everyone feels stress during the failure, relief when it is over, the maintenance staff feel like heroes and are sometimes rewarded. The result is a culture of reactive maintenance as there is no incentive to prevent the failures in the first place.

There have been a variety of maintenance strategies companies employ to 'control' the costs of maintenance. Changes to maintenance strategies and practices often do not see an immediate impact. Instead, the lag time in a program, positive or negative, is an average of 12 to 24 months before full benefits are seen. In maintaining assets, it is important to remember the coupled with the human or cultural aspect to any change.

Asset management, including those aspects of R&M related to it, offer an unexplored frontier for business to improve competitiveness. This opportunity exists regardless of existing programs and their success. It can be explored through understanding your assets, literally knowing what you own, and determining the best strategy for each one. The impact within the business, sometimes even through the lag period, can be staggering.

8.1 Cautions

Just using the term 'asset management' in the description of a program does not make the program a true asset management program. In the early days of the success of Lean and Re-Engineering, once the successes became published, many executives called for those programs to be implemented in their companies. The result was a suddenly sprouting of consulting firms that claimed to be able to provide such programs with little to no real experience. These programs had a tendency to fail miserably and sometimes very publicly. For instance, some would recommend just releasing personnel, shutting down departments or changing processes without a full understanding of how it works. The result was undermanned critical systems and departments.

8.2 The Development of an Asset Process

The development of a successful asset management program involves a process. Without a structured system, supported at all levels of the company, any such program will not succeed.

The first step of the process requires the identification of assets using an asset census. This allows the company to understand the equipment that they own and allows the process of selecting critical equipment. Critical equipment is selected based upon company criteria that are selected around:

- Safety and regulatory issues;
- Production-related equipment;

- Equipment that would be expensive to repair or replace; and,
- Other equipment priorities.

Once equipment has been prioritized, it can be processed based upon the greatest to least impact on the business. These are then put through a set of processes such as PM Optimization (PMO) and RCM to select the appropriate maintenance processes to manage the equipment. The results are optimized within the company ERP/EAM/CMMS system with old practices removed. The equipment condition is evaluated and baselines taken.

Other best practices are developed and maintenance processes reviewed for correctness. Processes such as RCA, repair versus replace, and others, also make up the suite of best practices that provide feedback into the process, which should be scheduled for maintenance effectiveness reviews periodically. In this process, the maintenance practices are reviewed to ensure that they meet their original intention and are modified as necessary.

8.3 What is the Impact of Asset Management

With the existing aging workforce and a decade long gap in the next largest workforce to enter the prime working age (Baby-Boomers made up approximately 78 million people in the USA while the newer Baby-Boom Echo generation will be over 100 million in the USA), companies have a prime opportunity to improve existing asset management practices. The improvement to any program, or lack of one, will have a direct impact on production throughput, inventory and operating costs as well as customer retention.

It is important to understand there is the possibility that some costs will increase during the implementation of asset management. However, on average, the following impacts are possible when moving to a condition-based maintenance versus reactive program:

- Reduction in maintenance costs of 24-30%
- Elimination of unplanned breakdowns by 70-75%
- Reduction in downtime of 35-40%
- Increase in throughput of 20-25%

- Reduction of PM's by 33-66%
- Man-hour improvements of 45-50%

The development of the program also requires the coordination of all parts of the company.

Asset management and R&M provide one of the last frontiers is business improvements. However, most companies approach the opportunity from the wrong direction and just make budget and personnel costs. The real opportunity is in controlling the business assets through an appropriate asset management process. The impact of the business while ensuring on-time deliveries to customers can make the difference in efforts to increase profits and competitiveness.